SWEET SORROW

Finding Enduring Wholeness after Loss and Grief

Sherry Cormier

ROWMAN & LITTLEFIELD
Lanham • Boulder • New York • London

Published by Rowman & Littlefield
An imprint of The Rowman & Littlefield Publishing Group, Inc.
4501 Forbes Boulevard, Suite 200, Lanham, Maryland 20706
www.rowman.com

Unit A, Whitacre Mews, 26-34 Stannary Street, London SE11 4AB

British Library Cataloguing in Publication Information Available

Library of Congress Cataloging-in-Publication Data Available

ISBN: 978-1-5381-1417-9 (cloth)
ISBN: 978-1-5381-1418-6 (electronic)

CONTENTS

Preface   vii

1 Introduction and Loss of the Fairy Tale   1
2 Sense of an Ending   5
3 The Veil of Illusion   17
4 The Transition and Aftermath   27
5 Manifestations of the Soul Following Death   37
6 Starting Over and Posttraumatic Growth   57
7 Turbulence and Change   65
8 Letting Go and Facing Loss: Stress and Self-Care   79
9 Coping with Loss: Grief Survivors   95
10 Responding to Loss: Grief Helpers   113
11 Health, Healing, and Hope   123

Epilogue: Jay   135
Contemplative Questions   141
Notes   143
Bibliography   155
Index   161
About the Author   169

PREFACE

I was approaching my sixth decade and feeling a keen delight about life. My parents were safely ensconced in a lovely retirement community in Illinois near my sister, my daughters were successfully exiting the nest, and my husband and I were enjoying a new home we had recently built, with some exciting travels amid our busy but fulfilling work schedules. I had no clue how dramatically my life was about to change.

Instead of entering this new stage of my life with my life partner and beloved family members, my sixties have been consumed with traumatic, stressful losses. My parents, husband, sister, and dog died, one following another, leaving myself and our daughters bereft. There were days, especially early on, after my husband, Jay, died, when I didn't know how I could go on without the presence of that big love. Although I'm a psychologist and had plenty of opportunities to study grief, the firsthand experience was far different from what I'd encountered from books, training, or even friends and clients walking their grief journey.

This book is my story of loss and healing, and yet it's so much more. It's about how we struggle and about how we manage. It's about how we *can* choose to wither or to grow when confronted with traumatic loss, and while it's my personal story, it's also a psychologist's perspective on how to endure and, ultimately, heal after loss.

Surprising Discoveries

The ten years since my husband, parents, and sister died have held many surprising discoveries, beginning with the fact that I could simultaneously lose so many people I loved and that I, and other survivors of hard loss, were able to cope better than imagined. Not everyone becomes stronger from traumatic loss, but a substantial number of trauma and loss survivors grow from challenging and catastrophic experiences in ways we couldn't have envisioned at the beginning of our bereavement journey. When loss came to me, I was amazed to discover how many of us don't stay stuck in despair but move forward and thrive. As a psychologist, I wanted to identify how this happens and share the process with others. I've learned it's not just one thing that propels us toward coping and thriving, but rather a constellation of ingredients I describe in *Sweet Sorrow*. Another big discovery was that while the physical body of our beloved is no longer around, their presence and spirit still surround us. While not everyone will experience this kind of connection with someone they've lost, being aware of this possibility may offer a new form of optimism or balm for the wound. *Sweet Sorrow* also provides solid suggestions, tips, and resources for the process of starting over, healing, and caring for self and others who are suffering.

Loss and Grief Come to Everyone

This book is also about the recognition that we aren't on this loss journey alone. The Buddhist story of the mustard seed illustrates this: A bereaved woman who had lost her only son couldn't put down his dead body and was going mad from the senselessness and meaninglessness of the experience. She encountered the Buddha and asked if he could bring her son back to life. His response was priceless:

"*Yes, I can,*" he said, "*if you bring me a mustard seed from a house that has not experienced death.*"

When the woman went from house to house and could find no one who hadn't experienced death, she put down her son's body to rest.

Pema Chodron, in *When Things Fall Apart*, says, "Sooner or later we're going to have an experience we can't control; the essence of life is that it's challenging . . . but to be fully alive, fully human, and completely awake is to be continually thrown out of the nest."[1] This is the conundrum. How do we cope with and heal from something so real, so pervasive, that we aren't ready to meet?

As we companion together throughout the book, you'll notice certain themes that have to do with positive coping and healing—from helplessness to empowerment, from hopelessness to hopefulness, from anxiousness to calm, and from sadness to joy.

Acknowledgments

There are many people who made the fruition of this book possible, beginning with the generosity of Anne Brooks, whom I met soon after I moved to Annapolis in a prosthodontic office waiting room. My writing group colleagues Anne, Libby Cataldi, Amanda Gibson, Amy Richter, Mary Luck Stanley, Nancy Jo Steetle, and Roberta Watts read and commented on successive chapter drafts. My writing coach and friend Laura Oliver, author of *The Story Within*, helped me bring my story to life on the written page. Her wisdom and acumen permeate throughout. And professional editor Randy Landenheim-Gill made my writing sparkle! Natalie Boonchaisri handled so many technical pieces so beautifully, allowing me to focus on the writing! And my serendipitous meeting with Sam Horn of the Intrigue Agency on Captain Jen's Windward Schooner proved to be the foundation of some terrific marketing advice she sent my way. It's been the honor of my lifetime to work with Rowman & Littlefield Publishers and my fabulous editor, Suzanne Staszak-Silva.

As a caveat, all names have been changed to protect the identity of the people described, with the exception of daughters and spouses.

Sherry Cormier
October 18, 2017

I

INTRODUCTION AND LOSS OF THE FAIRY TALE

I am not what happened to me, I am what I choose to become.[1]
—Carl Jung

Once in a while, in the middle of an ordinary life, love gives us a fairy tale.

Love gave me a fairy tale when I was forty-two years old and a thunderbolt arrived via a vibrant and handsome man named Jay. Eventually, Jay and I were married and for seventeen years experienced a mostly magical love story. Our marriage was extraordinarily intimate: physically, emotionally, and spiritually. We had been married before to good, decent people, yet something in our former marriages was missing for us, so we were committed to making our relationship as strong and as close as possible. The result was a connection at a deep, energetic level that felt as if it transcended time and space, a phenomenon that Jay and I described as "time away from time." We were also both psychotherapists. Because therapists are trained to share intimacies, we probably did have an unusual marriage. Of course we had our challenges, but through all of them, we never lost sight of our profound connection.

This book isn't about the story of our marriage, but its loss. A week after we celebrated our seventeenth anniversary, beloved, strong, healthy Jay was diagnosed with terminal esophageal cancer that had metastasized into nearby tissues and organs, making it inoperable. The surgeon who initially diagnosed the aggressive adenocarcinoma told me privately that Jay could be gone in six to twelve months despite treatment. True to his prediction, Jay died six months later. The fairy tale, it seemed, was over.

But was it? After his death, I experienced a number of profound connections with my beloved, mostly in the form of dreams that would wake me up in the night, allowing me to process and chronicle them. And one of the most important lessons I've learned with these connections is that while a life ends with death, a relationship lives on.

This book describes my journey from loss toward healing. Like our marriage, my journey with grief has also been intimate and unusual, perhaps mirroring the intimacy and singularity of the relationship Jay and I had in life. The experiences I discuss in this book are mine and mine alone and, of course, from a narrative viewpoint, reflect my subjective reality. And, with the exception of daughters and spouses, everyone else's name has been changed to preserve their privacy.

In the course of reading this book, you may feel surprised, skeptical, envious, or puzzled. This may be particularly true if you also have experienced a loss and have had a journey with grief that isn't similar to the one I share here. Let me reassure you, grief is grief, sadness is sadness, heartbreak is heartbreak; and there is no right or wrong way to grieve.

As a psychotherapist, I've had the privilege of working with many people who've suffered great losses. I've also shared stories with a number of close friends who've encountered difficult losses of their own. In listening to clients and friends, I'm struck by the variety of experiences people have with loss and grief. I know of someone who has visited her child's grave faithfully over a long number of years and yet hasn't experienced postdeath dreams about her child. I have a good friend who, on the other hand, has received a number of postdeath messages and connections with the brother she lost a few years ago. These two people have had very different grief journeys, yet each is as significant and as valid as the other.

I've found through my work and experience that one's journey with grief evolves on a continuum. And while some of us may have experiences that fall at one end, there is nothing wrong with being in the middle or at the other end entirely.

It's my hope that in reading this book you'll be able to find some consolation in your loss journey and that one day you'll realize some of your pain has lost its edge. Although there were many despairing days for me, when I wondered how I would survive, ultimately, I realized the best gift I could give Jay to honor his vibrant energy and joie de vivre was to carry on and make the most of my remaining time on earth.

For Jay, our daughters, and survivors of heartbreaking loss everywhere who feel impoverished in spirit, I dedicate this book to you.

2

SENSE OF AN ENDING

The only thing that lasts forever is now.[1]
—Paul Friday

On July 5, 2007, I accompanied my husband, Jay, to our community hospital, where he was scheduled for his first colonoscopy and upper endoscopy. At sixty-three, he had waited long past the prescribed age, fifty, for his first GI screening, which was much more about the upper part of his digestive system than the lower one. Recently, he'd noticed some difficulty in swallowing food and had even taken it upon himself to schedule a rare appointment with our family physician. Neither Jay nor the physician seemed that alarmed; the doctor noted that, with age, the esophagus often develops strictures. So on one hand, I wasn't alarmed, while on the other, I was suspicious. We all would have been much more uneasy if we'd known then what we heard several weeks later concerning the huge upswing in esophageal cancer among white men in their sixties in the United States.

Just the day before, on the Fourth of July, spent with our dear friends Jack and Joan at their mountain lake house, my husband joked, "Well, maybe I have esophageal cancer." This was no joking matter to me; my maternal grandfather had died from it. Six months earlier, when we were visiting Jay's daughter Laura, we'd rushed Jay to the emergency room with what turned out to be a kidney stone, and I had remarked to her, "I can't quite put my finger on it, but I'm concerned there's something going on with your dad."

Jay had developed a slight cough in the spring that we'd both attributed to allergies. Jay was a handsome man, with lots of dark hair and vibrant blue eyes that radiated warmth upon everyone who came in his path. Yet sometimes during that spring I'd seen him sitting outside on our deck, those vibrant blue eyes looking far away, as if a part of him was already vanishing to some unknown time and space. He developed another, more serious kidney stone that had to be surgically removed a month prior to his cancer diagnosis. This procedure had required a chest X-ray, and while I'd read the report, nothing at that time registered with me or with any of his physicians when it said there was some slight pleural effusion in his lungs. I didn't know enough then to realize that pleural effusion was something that needed a follow-up to determine its cause, which can range from a slight infection to cancer.

As the morning of July 5 ensued, though, I was upbeat, walking the halls of the hospital, even visiting the gift shop while the surgeon performed the colonoscopy and endoscopy on my husband. I knew the drill. You waited, you shopped, you drank a latte, and the doctor came to find you standing out in the hall to deliver the good news: "Everything went well."

So it should have been a red flag to me when this surgeon didn't come out in the hall to find me. Instead, a nurse came and said, "The doctor will see you now in Room A." Still, nothing about being alone in Room A with the doctor alarmed me. Not even the starkness of the windowless room, with its sterile white walls. I was unprepared when he said, "We did your husband's colonoscopy first and it was totally clear. But then we did the upper endoscopy into the esophagus and there's definitely something there."

"Something?" I asked querulously, repeating his word, perhaps not wanting to state the potentially obvious.

"Yes," he confirmed. "A tumor, a large tumor, and I'm sure it's malignant."

"Well," I challenged, "didn't you do a biopsy that gets sent out? How can you know without the pathology report?"

"We did do a biopsy and I am sure it will confirm that he has a large malignant tumor at the base of his esophagus. You need to make plans to follow up on this immediately," he stressed.

Working hard to maintain my composure with the physician, I went into problem-solving mode. "What do you recommend? Where would you start if this were your spouse?"

"I'll give you the name of a surgeon at the esophageal cancer center at University of Pittsburgh Medical Center [UPMC] and I'll send all the diagnostic reports up to him as well," he volunteered. "Your husband's immune system must be down because he is taking longer than usual to wake up from the sedation, but when he does, we'll come and find you so you can see him."

The First of Many Angels Appears!

I stumbled out of the room and walked blindly down the hospital corridor, trying to find a place where I could let the tears flow freely. By the time I got to the end of the hall, I crumpled. I was lost and frightened and I knew enough about esophageal cancer to feel pessimistic. Just the week before, in my yoga class, I'd learned of a clergy member in the community who'd been diagnosed with leukemia and died three weeks later. *This is how it's going to go down*, I thought to myself. *He's going to go quickly, will be gone in a flash, and I'll be left alone.* Just then, an older woman with the kind, open face of an angel walked by and touched my shoulder.

"Dear one," she said, "I have no idea what you're going through, but I can tell it's not good news, and I just want to give you a hug."

That was the first of many mercies showered on me through the kindness of strangers in the months to come. The sort of kindness that makes you dissolve even more because it penetrates the few defenses you have left. Now, years later, I can still feel the warmth of her hand on my shoulder, and I wish there was some way for this unnamed woman to know how much her random act of kindness meant to this struggling soul on that awful day.

Of course there were many details about what happened the rest of that day. How my husband woke up and asked me what had happened and, again, keeping my composure momentarily at least, my telling him matter-of-factly what the physician had reported. How I called our best friends, Jack and Joan, with whom we had shared the previous day at their lake house, when life still felt normal, to give them the news. How Jack dropped everything to rush over to the hospital to be with us and see what we needed. How on the drive home I called my hairdresser to cancel my appointment for the next day because I didn't know where we would be or what we would be doing in this journey of life now called Cancer.

AN UNFORGETTABLE CONVERSATION

By the time we arrived home, the sedation had worn off for Jay, and reality had kicked in for him, too. And the moments of stoicism on my part at the hospital had worn thin as well. We collapsed on our queen-size bed, even though it was only one in the afternoon and a weekday at that. A conversation ensued that burned a hole in me. It was one of those conversations you never forget that sears through you in such a way that it becomes embedded in who you are.

"If I were in your shoes," my husband said, "I would be so angry with me . . . I have been relationally irresponsible. I used to smoke a pipe, then I chewed tobacco, now I've eaten the wrong foods and gained weight; I've been overworking, stressed myself out, and been there for other people," he continued, "but I haven't been there for myself." All true, and also the classic dilemma for people like my husband and me who, as psychotherapists, were expert caregivers for others but novice caregivers for ourselves.

Wow! If we weren't discussing a potential end-of-life issue, I would have been elated by my husband's disclosure, his awareness of the impact of his actions on my life too. As it was, it just reinforced the sickening feeling in my stomach at the hospital that had continued to expand to the point of nausea. Moreover, I really didn't know how to respond to him. This was new territory for me. I felt some unspoken presumption that would color my reactions to Jay from that point forward: How do you allow yourself to be angry with someone who has cancer, and a life-threatening cancer at that? Finding a way to manage my own emotions during this journey without dumping them on my husband was one of my most important initial challenges. For me, this challenge was particularly daunting. I was a well-known psychotherapist in a very small town. I knew all the other therapists, some personally and some professionally. My husband and I had built our strong marriage on the precept of always turning to each other, but now that assumption seemed to shift for me.

I started to turn to my friends in much more significant ways than before, and I also made a serious commitment to the role of acupuncture and Chinese medicine in my life. I knew enough, perhaps too much, about the effect of chronic anger and sadness on the body, and at some level, as afraid as I was for Jay, I was also afraid for myself. I was all too aware of the journey of Christopher Reeve and his wife, Dana, who died soon after he did. The stats speak volumes: spouses often die within eighteen months of each other. Being the mother of two daughters who for various reasons depended on me emotionally and the daughter of two ninety-year-old parents, including a mother who was caregiver for my father, who suffered from advanced dementia, I knew I had to find a way to substantially take care of myself during this process.

I contacted my acupuncturist and began having regular acupuncture sessions. I knew I could also confide in my acupuncturist when my body was calling out for me to vent because he wasn't part of my local psychotherapeutic community of professional colleagues.

I also started spending time with friends, who began to play a more important role in my life. At times that felt like a mixed blessing. My closest friend called me several days after Jay's initial diagnosis. "You have to get out of the house," she said. "I'll come pick you up and we'll go out for a while."

She came by and took me to lunch and to one of our favorite stores, T. J. Maxx, which always had been a place the two of us loved to browse for great deals and good finds as part of our stress-reduction plan. But this time, being with her there was a disconnect for me. Walking around the store while she was elated and happy over material things made the pit in my stomach worse. Buying a new pair of shoes or finding some beautiful object for my house seemed pointless and trivial. I was feeling too discouraged to experience much joy. How could I enjoy myself ever again when I knew what my husband was facing, when I had a pretty good idea what would be in store for me, too, as a result?

Jay's Postcancer Diagnosis Birthday

The days that followed Jay's cancer diagnosis had a surreal quality to them. Jay's sixty-fourth birthday was July 9, four days after we spoke with the doctor. Our birthdays had always been special times of love and celebration for the two of us. We showered each other with cards, love notes, letters, small gifts, and marked the occasion in some special way, with an out-of-town weekend trip or dinner at a wonderful restaurant. Usually our birthday celebrations extended over the course of a week!

This year was different. I felt especially gloomy, wondering if this would be my husband's last birthday alive. Jay was slightly more optimistic, thinking the tumor might kill him eventually but believing he would have several years before that happened. This year we spent his birthday distracted. We were in the process of making telephone calls to family members and close friends, telling them about Jay's diagnosis and what it would mean. Jay was concerned about the potential impact his missing work would have on his multitude of clients in the group private practice where he was employed. He was preoccupied with what and how much to tell his clients and how to provide for continuity of services to them in his potential absence during procedures, tests, and chemotherapy. We were also apprehensive, anticipating our big trip to the University of Pittsburgh Medical Center esophageal cancer center in several weeks, at which time we would get a more definitive picture of the cancer and the potential treatment options. For both of us, it felt like that day couldn't arrive soon enough.

The UPMC Cancer Center Consultation

Eventually it did, and we made the first of many treks up the road to the UPMC Hillman Cancer Center, located in the trendy Shadyside neighborhood of Pittsburgh, a seventy-five-minute journey from our door in Morgantown, West Virginia, to theirs each way. On our first sojourn there, we chatted during the drive about what to expect. It was impossible to talk about anything other than cancer.

"Are you nervous?" I asked.

"Only about the PET scan. I wonder if I'll feel claustrophobic," he mused aloud.

One of the most challenging parts of Jay's diagnosis for me was managing my feelings about hospitals. I've never liked spending time in them, even as a visitor, and now I was finding myself actually having to hang out in hospitals as a regular part of my summer vacation from teaching at the university. The surgeon at UPMC wanted to perform several procedures on Jay's esophagus so he could see the tumor for himself. Additionally, the center wanted to do all the scans there so they could track the tumor's progression.

I dreaded walking through the halls of this place, where I knew every patient I encountered was someone with cancer. It felt intimidating. Some of that intimidation was mitigated, however, when we met the surgeon and his team. We felt welcomed and heard by the surgeon, who had such a hopeful and compassionate manner. Dr. McGuire, a Canadian, with a handsome, youthful face, had a wonderful slight accent to his rich-sounding voice. He also had just the right combination of wit and knowledge.

At that time the information available on the Internet about esophageal cancer was frequently omitted from lists of various kinds of cancers. It was so helpful that Dr. McGuire provided information about it that we hadn't found on any websites. Jay and I actually felt uplifted after meeting with Dr. McGuire and had some glimmer of hope as he talked about the potential of curing esophageal cancer. Of course, at that point none of the scans had been performed on Jay.

On the day of the procedures, I was ushered into a large waiting room while Jay was taken upstairs to the outpatient surgery area. Once again, I was nauseated with anticipation and fear. I managed my emotions with what I do best: talking with other people who are struggling. I struck up a conversation with a woman sitting next to me who was from a different part of West Virginia and whose husband, also diagnosed with esophageal cancer, was upstairs also having procedures performed by Dr. McGuire. She spoke of being stunned to discover her husband had cancer after anemia had been revealed in routine bloodwork the month before. Suspecting colon cancer, a surgeon had performed both upper and lower endoscopies; the upper one had shown esophageal cancer instead. "Oh!" I exclaimed. "My husband also had routine bloodwork a month ago and his blood panel was absolutely perfect! You're so lucky that something showed up in your husband's panel leading to an early diagnosis."

"Well," she said, "perhaps so, but I'm a nervous wreck about all this. Ever since my husband's diagnosis I've had to take tranquilizers."

I mustered my listening skills to help her discuss her anxieties while managing to quell my own. As always, in being able to focus on someone else's issues, mine faded into the background, providing at least momentary relief.

Discovering "Friday's Laws"

In addition, I shared with her a bookmark I had picked up at the UPMC cancer center bookstore called *Friday's Laws*, based on a book by Paul Friday, a PhD psychologist who worked for UPMC. I'd been reading the eight statements on the bookmark over and over, somewhat obsessively, I admit, using it as a mantra for coping with my own worries.

According to Friday's Laws,

> *Life is difficult.*
> *Perception is reality.*
> *Change is the toughest thing to do.*
> *You can never change someone else; you can only change yourself.*
> *While I am responsible for all that I say and do, I am not responsible for your response.*
> *The future and the past are seldom as good or as bad as we anticipate or remember.*
> *Nobody has a squeaky-clean psyche,* and
> *The only thing that lasts forever is—NOW.* [2]

That last phrase was really starting to resonate with me.

She and I were in both email and telephone contact over the next several years. One huge difference between us emerged eventually: her husband was cured, while mine died. There's a lot of science that goes into effective cancer treatment, but there's also a lot of luck, and her spouse had the luck, for sure.

The Roller-Coaster Ride Begins

Several weeks later, Jay and I once again went to UPMC to meet with Dr. McGuire and to obtain the results of all the procedures and scans.

The news wasn't encouraging and our initial hopefulness waned. We were now officially on the part of the journey I called the roller-coaster ride, and we reexperienced it many times during the next six months. Jay would rally or even go into remission and we would believe he could beat this disease, and then new symptoms or problems would emerge and we would feel pessimistic. It felt like we were living in a bipolar world full of ups and downs, with good news followed by dashed hopes and dreams. The PET scan revealed that Jay's cancer had progressed into his lymphatic system, making surgery an impossibility. Dr. McGuire indicated that in Japan, they might attempt a twenty-hour surgery in this situation but he didn't recommend it. He wanted to manage Jay's cancer with chemotherapy and perhaps radiation. He didn't say Jay's cancer wasn't considered curable; in fact, he remained optimistic that a combination of chemotherapy and radiation might shrink the tumor enough that the disease could be managed for a while as a chronic process.

The oncologist we were assigned to, Dr. Grover, a recent transplant from Johns Hopkins and another middle-aged, high-energy, and very approachable fellow, was blunter. He said something to us that was so penetrating that even now the memory of his words shake me as he told us that while chemotherapy could shrink the tumor, that eventually at some undetermined time, the tumor would kill him. He went on to add that from the reports and scans he had read, he believed Jay's tumor had been present for the last four years. That fact was startling. Except for some slight things I'd noticed in the six months or so before his diagnosis, Jay would have been the last person I ever would have thought had cancer. He looked healthy, was hardly ever sick, and was a robust and vibrant person who at an earlier age ran both the Boston and the New York marathons and many more on a regular basis. There was no history of cancer in his family and his yearly physicals and blood panels showed no abnormal readings of any kind. When we explained all this to Dr. Grover, he gazed at us with the utmost kindness and caring in his eyes while stating that Jay was way too young to have his life taken away by some awful kind of cancer that rarely was detected early enough for a cure.

The plan was for Dr. McGuire and Dr. Grover to oversee Jay's treatment but that the treatment itself would be implemented by our local cancer center in Morgantown. Neither of us had discussed any other options either between ourselves or with our adult daughters. We were fortunate to have an accredited cancer center in our town in West Virginia and to be only about seventy miles away from the thirteenth-ranked hospital in the country where they were overseeing Jay's case. Monday morning quarterbacking is common in instances when someone doesn't recover from an illness. In retrospect, perhaps getting another opinion about Jay's status from an out-of-state facility that specialized only in cancer treatment might have been useful. At the same time, perhaps another perspective may only have added to our confusion. And we were also being pragmatic given our financial situation. If we had a million dollars and neither of us needed to work, would we have explored temporarily moving closer to a place like MD Anderson in Texas or Sloan Kettering in New York for treatment? Perhaps so. Yet we valued spending the time we had with our friends and community and being in our beautiful new home, which brought us both great joy and peace. Staying in Morgantown also allowed our adult daughters and Jay's out-of-town friends to make frequent visits.

The WVUH Cancer Center and Initial Chemotherapy

The next part of the roller-coaster ride involved going to our university-based cancer center and meeting with the GI oncologist there, who would manage the administration of the chemotherapy recommended by the UPMC team. When we met Dr. Michaud, Jay and I fell in love with him. Here was a physician who had such great compassion it exuded from him. We were immediately struck by his soft-spoken, kind yet competent and confident communication and demeanor, immediately putting us at ease and feeling grateful to be in his care. Obviously a seasoned professional with his shock of graying hair, he gently and thoroughly explained the process of chemotherapy, noting the potential benefits and risks. A matter emerged that was of great concern to us. He happened to remark that we would be dealing with esophageal cancer that has metastasized to the lungs. He mentioned it because he said you can live without any organ in some fashion except your lungs!

I think we were both stunned by this news since we had not heard this said so directly at UMPC and, once again, the roller coaster took another drop to the bottom.

We set up Jay's full-day chemotherapy treatments at the end of the week so he had the weekends to recover before seeing clients on Mondays. I don't think it ever occurred to either of us to handle things any differently. Both of us were comforted by our routines. There was some semblance of normalcy in getting up and doing what we were used to doing in the face of the disruption of routines spending Fridays at the WVU Cancer Center for chemotherapy, with many trips in between for bloodwork monitoring and injections to keep Jay's white blood cell count from getting dangerously low, a side effect of the chemo.

The day of the first chemotherapy treatment arrived before we knew it. We felt especially anxious and afraid, having heard many horror stories about chemo despite Dr. Michaud's reassuring communications and explanations. We put a plan in place that we thought would be helpful to both of us because this was going to be an all-day affair. Jay was going in early in the morning with our next-door neighbor who worked at the hospital and would take him to the cancer center. This would give me time to meditate and get some things accomplished before going over to the hospital. Our friend Jack was going to arrive for the morning shift and stay with Jay during the first part of the chemo administration. I was coming over later to stay for the afternoon shift and to drive Jay home.

When I arrived and saw Jay midway through the chemo injection, I felt very faint. His face was yellow, I assumed from the toxicity of the drugs to the liver. When I witnessed the precautions taken by the chemo administration nursing staff handling the chemo IV, such as the gloving up and the extreme care not to touch any of the solution, I was also greatly concerned. What unknown effects would this poison have on him if it was considered this toxic by those administering it? Gradually, though, my anxiety diminished as I listened to the beautiful music drifting around us, played by a harpist sitting in the center of the chemotherapy suite. My anxiety was further reduced by the presence of wonderful Dr. Michaud, who made rounds checking on his chemo patients. His quietly confident yet unassuming manner was reassuring to even the most worried of patients and caregivers. Furthermore, I felt so comforted by the nursing staff, who provided countless hours of explanations about what was going on then and what to expect afterward.

Sleep, Sunset, and Laughter Caps the Day

When we arrived home at the end of the initial treatment with explicit instructions about the potential ramifications of the drugs and how to deal with them, as well as an ample supply of antinausea pills, we were simply relieved to have made it through the first of many rounds of chemo. It was late afternoon and, drained and exhausted, we dropped on our bed and took a nap, relaxing in each other's arms and in the comfort of knowing we were both still alive and had survived the journey, at least so far.

Nothing could have prepared me, or Jay for that matter, for what ensued after we woke up from our nap. The quiet, sallow-looking Jay had been transformed. The color was back in his face and, moreover, he had a spark to his step and a lilt in his voice. It was early evening in the summertime and the sun glowed copper in the sky as it moved toward its westernmost point before setting. "Let's go outside," he said. "I've been cooped up inside all day. I want to feel the sun on my face."

We joined hands and practically skipped outdoors. I couldn't believe what I was witnessing. He had more energy than I had seen in weeks. Later, I would learn this was chemical, induced by the huge amounts of steroids given to him at the end of the chemo treatment. But for the time being, I enjoyed having my husband back, buoyed by his own joy-filled, youthful spirit. As we stood on our front porch, surveying our beautiful summer landscaping, with the side rose garden in full, resplendent bloom, our close friends and neighbors down the street drove past the house.

Seeing us outside, they stopped and got out of the car. Jay had become somewhat withdrawn from people since his initial cancer diagnosis, so they weren't sure what to expect. He bounded over to them as if he hadn't seen them in years and exclaimed with great happiness, "Look! I got through my first chemo therapy and I feel great!" They, like me, were astounded by the change in his demeanor and behavior. They stayed and talked for a while, and what I remember most about that evening is hearing my husband laugh again. It had been a few weeks since I had heard his full-hearted belly laugh, which I had grown accustomed to hearing regularly BC (before cancer). When we went to bed that night, the roller coaster began rising toward the top. Of course, from where we were then, we couldn't see the other side of the hill.

3

THE VEIL OF ILLUSION

The recognition of an illusion is also its ending. Its survival depends
on your mistaking it for reality. [1]
—Eckhart Tolle

After Jay began his chemo treatments, we settled into a rhythm or,
perhaps more accurately, we settled into an illusion. With each passing
treatment, he appeared to be getting better and better, even though I
realize now the appearance of good health was a mirage. After three
chemo treatments, he finally was able to eat again, to swallow soft solid
food. The persistent cough he had experienced since early spring,
which we had attributed to allergies, was waning. He was, for the most
part, working full time, seeing his myriad of daily clients, while I was
teaching, seeing clients, and writing my textbook. Moreover, he had a
lot of increased energy. We were fortunate to be in the throes of an
Indian summer, the afternoons uncharacteristically warm and sunny.
We took full advantage of the persistently great weather, going out on
our small rowboat at the lake, biking the trails, hiking, gardening, and
sitting out in the sun. Jay, in particular, spent a lot of his free hours
napping on our back deck overlooking the woods, listening to the water-
fall and soaking in the gradually changing colors of the leaves from
green to crimson.

Jay felt well enough to do some short weekend travel and also to
entertain visits from his two daughters. My eldest daughter and my
granddaughter, who was turning two, lived the closest of the four
daughters, and we were able to make a few trips there. Jay's endorphins

seemed to rise with every contact with little Shelby. On one of those magical visits, she completely snubbed her mother in favor of spending time with her Yay, as she called him, and her Ahma, as she calls me. She inserted herself between us on the sidewalk and placed her left hand in Jay's right and her right hand in my left. Each time we came to a curb we would lift her up and she would yell "whee," "whee," and "whee." This pattern persisted at every curb and even today, Shelby insists she remembers those special walks with Yay and Ahma and calling out "whee."

We made one trip to Annapolis in late September for my youngest daughter Lisanne's twenty-fifth birthday celebration. We were mesmerized by the hues of brilliant orange and red on the trees along the mountains of western Maryland and then seduced by Annapolis, where the sun was hot and the air was salty from the breezes off the water. We met Chris, who recently has become Lisanne's husband. We liked him immediately and, in the course of conversation, discovered that his parents lived in a suburb north of Detroit directly across the street from where my parents had once lived. When my parents moved, Chris had just been born, and my parents had passed on the high chair they had bought for my daughters to Chris's parents for him to use!

Cracks in the Illusion

The illusion of Jay's health was alive and well, but intermittently, I saw some cracks in it, and the Annapolis trip was one of them. We hadn't spent any real time in Annapolis for several years and the small town had blossomed into what appeared to be an urban area, complete with six-lane highways and a burgeoning town-center shopping mecca. Jay appeared to be overwhelmed by it and wanted to sit outside in the sun while I navigated my way around town alone. That evening, on our way back to the hotel from Lisanne's birthday celebration, we got lost. Jay was driving and had a complete meltdown in the car. He said angrily, "We keep going around and around in circles. I don't like this town. I just wanna get back to our hotel." Finally, I insisted that he pull over to the curb and let me drive. Although some of the roads were new, I had a general feel for how to get around and believed I could eventually find our way back to our hotel, which I did.

All in all, it was an idyllic late summer and early fall. In early October we went to Columbus for a counseling conference, where I attended sessions and had meetings with my textbook editor. Coincidentally, Lee, my editor, had recently been diagnosed with advanced breast cancer and, like Jay, has since passed on. During our dinner meeting, instead of the usual discussion about the textbook, our conversation centered on cancer. I can't say who was more excited to have that conversation, Lee or Jay. It was as if the two of them were enjoying a cancer-support meeting during dinner. Lee had a glass of wine with dinner and complained, "I'm limited now to one glass of wine with dinner. I hate not being able to drink more wine. What a pain. But they think that some amount of alcohol fuels breast tumors."

Jay complained about his daily juice drinks: "Lee, less wine isn't too bad. But these God-awful vegetable juice drinks I have every day from organic kale and beets and garlic don't taste very good. But I've been told these are a good way to get energy into my healthy cells."

A FINAL VISIT WITH MY DYING DAD

Just as we were wrapping up dinner, and laughing a lot in the process, I got a phone call from my sister, who lived in Illinois. My parents, both approaching ninety, had moved out there several years before. "Sherry," she said, "I hate to tell you this. I know how hard your life is right now with what's going on with Jay. But Daddy is dying. Mother called hospice in and they said you better get out here as he has a week or maybe less to live." We left Columbus early the next morning to drive back to Morgantown, where I repacked my bags, made arrangements for my classes and clients, and got on the next plane to Illinois. I was acutely aware during this trip of making it by myself. Jay and I had visited my parents shortly before his cancer diagnosis—together. Now I was on my own. I tried to steel myself on the plane. My sister had told me that my father hadn't eaten much for several weeks and was skin and bones. I wondered how it would be to see him like that. Daddy had developed dementia about ten years before, following an emergency surgery. But my dad never forgot me, and whenever I visited, he clearly knew I was there and who I was. I wondered if this time would be different.

When I arrived late in the afternoon, my mom immediately took me into the bedroom. Daddy was emaciated and seemed to be in agonizing pain, writhing around in the bed. But as soon as he heard me say, "Hi, Daddy, its Sherry," he straightened himself out. He couldn't speak but simply put his hands together and clapped and clapped and clapped. To this day, this memory brings me to tears.

I asked my mother when the hospice folks had last checked on Daddy and she said it had been when they were there for the initial visit. I said, "Mom! Something is wrong with this picture. Can't you tell Daddy is in pain? Please call them and have them come over right away!" My mother, who never liked to *bother* anyone, resisted initially but finally did call and was told they were busy with other patients but would get there as soon as they could, perhaps later that day or the following one.

My dad seemed agitated for a while longer, but mercifully fell into a deep and peaceful rest. When I came into his room the next morning, I knew he had passed during the night. We called hospice immediately, but they didn't arrive to check the body or call in the death until early afternoon. This adverse experience with in-home hospice became cataloged in my mind. I made a mental note to myself that if Jay ever got to that point, we would be going a different end-of-life route, even though I knew this particular hospice was an exception to the norm. But this experience of witnessing the end of my dad's life was traumatic, and I couldn't even consider the possibility of having something like it happen to my beloved husband.

I stayed in Illinois for a week to help my mom. I wasn't that worried about Jay at the moment because he had been responding so well to the chemo. I had hope for him. But losing my dad was devastating, and when I returned to Morgantown, I felt physically and emotionally drained. The day after I returned, a Sunday, Jay and I sat on our covered porch. It was still warm and sunny outside, but I was cold and dark on the inside. I sobbed for several hours, feeling alone and overwhelmed with a sadness I couldn't shake.

THE VEIL OF ILLUSION

CHEMO'S DIRTY LITTLE SECRET

Jay continued to respond extremely well to the chemo. He was not experiencing awful side effects from the chemo, especially not physical ones. But increasingly there were emotional side effects I noticed. Much like the meltdown I'd witnessed in Annapolis, he had others. It felt to me as if he had a very short fuse and little things seemed to set him off and much of his frustration often got dumped on me. I kept reminding myself that we usually treat those we love the most the harshest—maybe because we feel safest with them. But one morning in particular, I was at my limit, no doubt in part because of my emotional fragility after losing my father. Jay had become frustrated with me and used some expletives. I called the cancer center in tears. I explained what was happening and asked what I could do. I was met with a very sympathetic voice on the other end of the line. She said, "Oh honey, I am so sorry. We see and hear this all the time with family members. Just hang in there." I wasn't sure if hanging in there was the most helpful piece of advice she could have given, but I did feel some strength in her assertion that this is quite common and I was not alone in what I was noticing and experiencing. However, I wondered why there was so little discussion about this by the physicians and the nursing staff. There were many warnings and cautions about physical side effects of chemo but very little was mentioned about emotional side effects. I felt like this was part of chemo's "dirty little secret." As a psychologist, I was trained to deal with emotional issues. It made me wonder how typical family members who didn't have the benefit of my training or discussion from the medical community handled this. Did they suffer in silence? Resort to self-medication with cigarettes or alcohol? Turn to family, friends, or their minister?

I surmised that some part of Jay was resentful that he was sick and I was well. But, in addition to that, I suspected the chemo was having some kind of powerful hold on the parts of his brain that processed emotional regulation, leaving him vulnerable and unregulated, much like a child. Perhaps when you put that kind of poison into your body it is not only toxic to your cancer and healthy cells, but also to your emotional well-being as well. Now I also understand that chemotherapy is very toxic to the liver as well.

In recent months, the cancer-treatment community has begun to address the psychological, social, and financial impacts of cancer care on patients, with the emerging field of psychosocial oncology that incorporates social support, mindfulness, and exercise in comprehensive cancer treatment programs. Currently, palliative care teams who include counselors and psychologists are primarily in the Department of Veterans Affairs. In August 2017, the American Psychological Association on Palliative Care and End-of-Life Issues issued a call for psychology's involvement in palliative and end-of-life care, noting that such involvement includes assistance for oncology physicians and family members as well as for patients.[2]

THE ILLUSION OF REMISSION!

In early November, we had a three-month follow-up with the oncologist at UPMC complete with a full-body PET scan. At this point in time, our illusion around Jay's health was the strongest because he appeared so robust and his scan was so good, making us feel he would defy the odds. When we arrived at the cancer center, it was impossible to tell that Jay had cancer. He looked well, he seemed well, he behaved well, and his PET scan showed no visible signs of cancer! When Dr. Grover came in the room where we were waiting and first looked at Jay, the first words out of his mouth were, "Do you feel as good as you look?" Jay grinned, a big, wide, sloppy grin that went across his face from one ear to the other ear, and said resoundingly, "YES." It was kind of astonishing. Both of us felt Jay looked better than Dr. Grover, who appeared fatigued despite his usual dose of humor. And as usual, there was a caveat. Dr. Grover explained that although the PET scan showed no visible signs of cancer, some cancer cells were microscopically too small to be detected on even these sophisticated scans, so it was likely that they were still lurking somewhere, undetected, in the body. Still, Dr. Grover was overjoyed about Jay's tremendous response to his chemo regimen and when we left his treatment room, we felt as though Jay's progress had given Dr. Grover a huge boost for his day. We also met with the surgeon managing Jay's case, and he suggested Jay return in December for a new procedure he would perform to open up his esophagus so that he could eat more solid foods.

This news was a terrific birthday gift to me. My birthday was a week after this visit to Pittsburgh. We had celebrated in part while in Pittsburgh, having dinner and wine in a small, romantic Italian restaurant for which Pittsburgh is known best with some mouthwatering homemade butternut squash pasta and tiramisu. We also had gone to Whole Foods where Jay had bought a beautiful purple Dendrobium orchid plant, my favorite, in honor of my birthday. This turned out to be the last plant Jay ever bought for me. This orchid plant lived for seven more years and continued to bloom at the most auspicious times, usually during the anniversary of Jay's passing, our wedding anniversary, and my birthday.

Thanksgiving came on the heels of my birthday and we had a quiet holiday at home, anticipating a house full of company for the Christmas holiday. It remains one of my most cherished memories with Jay. Because he was still feeling well and the weather was unusually good, we were able to walk in the woods, go see a movie, go out to dinner, and at his prodding, hang up outdoor Christmas decorations and put together a toy kitchen for Sierra's Christmas visit. We cooked an amazing Thanksgiving dinner and invited our neighbor Maureen, on call that day at the hospital, to join us. We slept in, took naps, watched movies in bed, listened to our favorite music, and slow danced to Chris Botti's *When I Fall in Love*. This holiday is especially memorable to me because it was the last of so many good things before Jay's health took a downturn, including the final time we made love.

The Illusion of Control

There was no chemo treatment the week of Thanksgiving so Jay missed a routinely scheduled treatment that week though neither of us thought that much about it. After all, we were living an illusion and hope was high. Jay was rescheduled for chemo the following Friday after Thanksgiving. But when that day arrived and he went to the cancer center for his routine bloodwork prior to chemo, he called me to say he had taken matters into his own hands and was going to take a chemo break. He strode out of the blood-drawing room where he asserted that his fellow cancer travelers cheered him on. He told me he got in his car and went to Dick's Sporting Goods store and T. J. Maxx to do some shopping.

As a psychologist, his behavior made perfect sense to me. After all, given all the blood testing, the chemo IV all-day drips, the shots following the chemo to keep his white blood cell count high, the self-injections he administered into his abdomen as well, the trips to an assortment of physicians, anyone would feel so worn down by this that seizing control in this manner would be empowering. But as his wife, I was afraid and angry. He had already missed a week of chemo due to Thanksgiving and now he wanted to miss the rescheduled treatment and how many more? Dr. Grover had built in a break after six full cycles of chemo but Jay had not yet completed six full cycles of chemo. He had completed only four. About a week later, he went back for another blood test and his cancer antigen number had risen alarmingly. Not all cancer centers use such blood tests as they are not particularly accurate, but the astonishingly quick rise of this number in such a short period of time gave me a huge sense of foreboding. In addition, Jay appeared to have some difficulty swallowing once again.

THE BEGINNING OF THE END

I put in a call to the surgeon at UPMC to discuss the situation. He suggested that we come to UPMC as soon as possible so he could perform the photodynamic therapy procedure which would open up Jay's esophagus and allow him to eat easily again. We arrived at UPMC about one week before Christmas, believing that we would be there for a night or two. However, after the procedure was performed, Jay did not bounce back. He had trouble getting out of bed. He said, "Oh honey, I don't know what's wrong but I feel like I have a terrible case of the flu. I ache all over and I don't feel like getting out of bed at all." My apprehension only increased in hearing him say this.

I sought out the head nurse on the floor at UPMC. I said: "I feel so worried about my husband. I feel like he is dying." She did not concur with my assessment that Jay was dying, although as an afterthought, she indicated that of course I knew him better than anyone.

Jay continued to spiral downhill the longer he stayed in the hospital. Later, when I queried the same nurse about his status and asked if this was typical, she said, "No. Usually patients feel great after this procedure and are up and about and on their way home the next day." Jay's lungs started to build up with fluid and he had a lot of trouble breathing and required oxygen. Not only that, but the physician had to come in periodically and drain his lungs so he could breathe again. However, none of the medical team seemed as alarmed as I felt. No one suggested restarting chemo nor did anyone suggest getting any new scans. Two days before Christmas, I drove back to Morgantown with the understanding that Jay's daughter and son-in-law would come the following day and drive him home for the Christmas holiday. On the day I left, Dr. Grover, the UPMC oncologist, saw Jay and according to Jay told him that the cancer was probably back and that after the holidays, he should return for rescans and resumption of the same or different chemotherapy. The UPMC surgeon recommended adding some radiation after the holidays as well. The next day when Jay arrived home in Laura and Steve's car, he couldn't get out of the car and down the steps into his man cave area without assistance. Additionally, since the time of his "clear" scan only seven weeks earlier, he looked as if he had aged about twenty years. The veil of illusion was developing some serious holes in its fabric.

4

THE TRANSITION AND AFTERMATH

Winter exhales. Her arctic breath blows lacy white frosting onto shivering nude trees. Her polar hands swirl vanilla iced cream glaze atop frigid waters and Earth's barren canvas.[1]
—Margaret V. Savage

Thanksgiving was idyllic, but Christmas was a sharp contrast due to Jay's deteriorating condition. My two daughters and granddaughter arrived from Pennsylvania and Maryland, but it was hard to enjoy them because of my growing concern about my husband. Just ten days before, he'd entered UPMC looking young and vibrant. He'd not lost any of his thick dark hair from chemo, his eyes shone brightly, and his color was good. Now he looked like an old, dying man. There was an odd yellowish pallor to his skin. His eyes had dulled. He had so much difficulty breathing, it was challenging for him to move around. He stayed glued to his brown suede recliner with his feet up, his eyes often closed. I can't imagine the amount of energy it took for him to endure the festivities, especially Christmas Day, with gift exchanges and games with our two-year-old granddaughter. Even her presence this time failed to cheer him. I did my best to hold it together for our family, but I was heartbroken. I knew there would never ever be another holiday for him. By New Year's Eve day, I was gravely concerned. He was almost gasping for breath and his vomiting had grown more constant.

January: A New Year but the Last Month

I called the UPMC surgeon who was in charge of managing his case. After talking to his attending and discovering Dr. McGuire was out of town, I contacted Jay's oncologist at the WVU Cancer Center. I was put through immediately to Dr. Michaud, who indicated Jay needed to be admitted to the hospital. I concurred. We needed support and backup and we needed it right away! To Dr. Michaud's credit, he found a way to bypass the emergency room so that Jay could be admitted directly to the ninth-floor cancer ward. The immediate challenge was to get him from the lower level of our home, up the steps, and out to the car. Fortunately, my youngest daughter's boyfriend Chris was able to assist. By the time we arrived at the hospital, got Jay into a room, and he'd had a scan, it was midnight. New Year's Eve. Never had I felt more lonely and sad. I knew what the New Year was bringing and it wasn't welcome news. It was no surprise to me when the oncology attending MD brought me into the room to look at the scan results on a monitor and said, "His lungs are shutting down. He has a month to live." My mood darkened, although I'd already known deep in my body that his life was almost over.

January was an event-filled month that moved quickly, but often it felt as if things occurred in slow motion. January weather in Morgantown is cold, gray, and icy. Things were declining for Jay. He got rescanned, which showed more metastases to his brain and, more alarmingly, to his pericardium. The latter necessitated another surgical procedure, performed by the head of cardiology. He asked my permission to have medical students view the procedure because it was an unusual one. I gave it instantaneously. I was grateful for the unbelievable care Jay was getting at our WVU hospital and willing to do whatever I could to repay my debt of gratitude. As one of my colleagues said, "WVUH physicians are known for their seasoned clinical expertise." So true, and we were the constant beneficiaries of their clinical acumen.

As luck would have it, Dr. Michaud was the oncology attending on call for the month of January. He never failed to stop by Jay's room at least once, sometimes twice daily. We were also fortunate that month to have a head resident in oncology, Dr. Laghari, who was from India. He also checked in with us several times a day. His bright smile, flashing dark eyes, and glistening white teeth always lifted our spirits.

Jay was on the ninth-floor cancer unit for about a week. I felt fortunate we'd never had to be on this ward before. Of all the places I'd been in both hospitals, this was the most depressing to me because there was so little life-force energy there. After Jay's pericardium procedure, he was on the cardiac unit, which felt better to me because it was about heart energy and not necessarily terminal illness.

End-of-Life and Palliative Care Decisions

As Jay's condition stabilized with excellent hospital care, we had to make a decision about end-of-life care. The hospice folks came around and lobbied for in-home hospice care. They made a strong argument, but my recent experience with my father was ever present for me. In addition, Jay's lungs were failing. He couldn't breathe without oxygen. Every day, as I climbed into bed next to him and pressed my hands into his back, I could feel the diminishment. He had so many medical issues, I felt incompetent to help make him pain-free and comfortable. And even though I believed the local hospices were compassionate and competent, it was also the depths of winter. We lived out of town in the middle of roads that weren't cleared of ice and snow, especially when there were school snow days. I was concerned about being able to get Jay back to the hospital on my own if necessary and about the ability of hospice workers to get to our house under certain road conditions.

So, with the help of Dr. Michaud and the excellent palliative care team at WVUH, we transitioned Jay into the skilled nursing unit at the hospital, which would serve as his inpatient hospice situation. This was a decision that proved to be so fabulous in every way that I've never second-guessed the wisdom of it. Because most of the other patients in the unit were recovering from things like orthopedic surgery, the unit always had a positive feel to it. It was managed efficiently but sensitively. The staff were so loving and gentle with my beloved. The unit contained a large community room with a kitchen, so when visitors and our daughters came, they had another place to sit and get coffee, water, or a snack. Jay's workplace was within walking distance of the hospital, which made it easy for his colleagues to come to discuss client-related issues and continuity of care since it was now evident he wouldn't be able to return to work. Finally, the accessibility of the location enabled

Jay to have much more contact with visitors than he would have had in our home, especially on snowy days.

A Poignant, Remembrance-Filled Final Visit Home

As Jay's condition stabilized, with the help of our friends Jack and Joan, he made one final visit home. Outside the sky was gray, almost ashen, and the trees behind our house were stripped bare of leaves. Snowflakes were whirling around the air with just a dusting on the ground. There were enough of them to create some light against the dark sky. I had prepared the house, putting on the fire and our favorite music and getting the hot water ready for tea, which I knew Jay could keep down. Jack and Joan respectfully gave us some time alone after they managed to get Jay out of their car and into the house along with his portable oxygen tank. We knew this would be his last visit home, and my recollection of the bittersweet tenderness of it even now makes me weep. We sat by the fire, sipping our tea, listening to the music, and reminisced about our fairy tale life together. Jay affirmed his love for me: "Honey, I've never loved anyone like I've loved you, and even though we've had some challenges, we are such a good fit." We were both weeping, Jay recalling the moment when he said to me, "I don't know how, or when, or where, but I know we will be together for life." When he said this, I was taken back to the day and place when he'd first made the comment before we were married. I figured he meant one day we would be in a position to be life partners. Now I understood he wasn't just talking about our life and connection here on earth, but in the realm beyond as well.

Emotional Healing and the Transition Arrives

While Jay's physical health was continually getting worse, his emotional health was consistently getting better. Perhaps because he had "detoxed" from all the chemo he hadn't had since mid-November, his bad moods and irritability disappeared. It was almost as if while the lack of chemo had spurred the tumor growth, it had stabilized his emotional health. Or maybe it was because, knowing he was dying, he became accepting and peaceful. He was a great follower of Byron Katie's work in *Loving What Is*, as she says, "I'm a lover of what is, regardless."[2]

By the last week of January, I knew his days were numbered. I think he did, too. At one point, he said to me, "I can feel my world getting smaller and smaller." And so it was on a Sunday evening, after his two daughters had left and my daughter Christiane and her boyfriend Jon had gone after bringing him a favorite Italian salad, that I felt in my gut *this is it.* I stayed with him very late that evening, then went home to get some sleep that was unusually disturbed. I woke up with a start at 6 a.m. and called the unit. The nurse said, "He had a challenging night." I dressed quickly, called Jack and Joan, and drove to the hospital.

As soon as I got to Jay's room and saw him, I realized he was in the active dying phase. He couldn't talk coherently. I ran upstairs to the residents' room—by now I knew the hospital by heart—and found Dr. Laghari before he started morning rounds. "Dr. Laghari, please, please come with me to Jay's room. Something is really off with him. I'm pretty sure he's dying now." He came with me immediately to assess Jay's condition and concurred that death was imminent. He gave some additional orders to the nursing staff. I called Jay's daughter though knowing she was several hours away; I was unsure whether she would get there before he passed.

Jack and Joan arrived and the nursing staff discreetly closed our door and didn't bother us again unless I went out to make a request. The three of us shepherded Jay through the transition from life on earth to the other side. He was still using an oxygen mask, but for the last hour of his life he shoved it off, as if to say, *I want to do this on my own terms!* I lay in bed next to him, caressing him, grateful for all the pain medication the staff administered, allowing him to make this journey in a completely different fashion than the one I'd witnessed with my father several months earlier. Jack and Joan were talking with him: "Jay, move toward the tunnel of light." Jay was always and completely at peace. After a few hours, he opened his eyes once, exhaled, and closed them. Then his spirit left his body to surround us with his grace.

He had transitioned on the twenty-eighth day of the month of January. The word "January" comes from Janus, the god of two faces, also known as the god of doorways—the god that looks both behind and ahead simultaneously. Like Janus, I knew now what was behind me, but I was stepping into unknown territory ahead. After Jay died, as peaceful and as spiritual as it was, I found myself quaking, as if the earth was shifting beneath my feet. I had survived a grueling six months of chemotherapy with him, diagnostic tests, trips to the local hospital and to the Pittsburgh cancer center, and through it all, I had been a warrior. Even as my husband lay dying next to me, his head on my shoulder, I was in control. But now he was gone.

The Arrival of Three Angels

Moments after he passed, three visitors, not having heard the news, entered the room as if following divine orders: Jay's minister, Tim, followed by our next-door neighbor, Saint Maureen as we called her, and my lifelong friend Patty. We formed a circle around his body. We held hands and Tim said a blessing and a prayer. I don't recall the words; I just remember being deeply moved—awed that all the right people had showed up at the same time, as if shepherded into the room by some unnamed force.

We stayed in the room and talked, but soon the head nurse came in. Jay had donated his body for medical research. She approached me gently, her hand on my arm. "I'm so sorry," she said. "All of us who helped take care of Jay loved him so much and we know this is a hard time for you, but it's about time for us to come in and wrap the body."

"Okay," I responded resolutely.

"Are you sure you're ready?" asked Jack and Joan, who had been with me all morning. "This will be your last chance to see his face."

"I know, and I have the moment inscribed indelibly on my brain, so yes. I'm ready."

As they took his body away, we talked as I gathered his belongings. Several of the staff came in to hug me and express their condolences. Jay's daughter Laura and her husband Steve arrived from Ohio just moments after they took Jay's body away. We described the morning to them, and I know they were able to absorb the warmth of the visitors surrounding us.

Debriefing with Friends and Family in the January Sunshine

We wandered out into the sunshine on a beautiful Monday afternoon. By this time, other friends and work colleagues had arrived, gone to the hospital coffee shop, and brought me a homemade raspberry scone and a hot, frothy cappuccino. I'd been at the hospital since 6 a.m. with little to eat. The coffee and scone melted in my mouth as I recounted the day to each new visitor, compelled by the need to share the momentous experience I was struggling to process. Adrenaline was still surging through my body from the intense events of the day. "All our daughters were here yesterday, and last night I had a feeling they wouldn't see him alive again. And when I got to the hospital again very early, after talking to the charge nurse, I could tell Jay was leaving us. It was so moving, so spiritual, as if we were shepherding him during this transition. It had an otherworldly quality to it," I explained.

The people surrounding me, listening to my story, all had been on the cancer voyage with us over the last six months. They'd called. They'd brought food. They'd come to the hospital daily during the last month to visit and to help.

Eventually, the sunlight turned into shadows as late afternoon approached. I was still outside on the bench, alone now, sipping a cappuccino and inhaling a second scone as I started making calls to family members to report the dreaded news. Holding myself together, I inhaled, then exhaled deeply before calling my eldest daughter first, knowing her teaching day would now be over. "Honey, Jay passed today," I said tentatively, sniffling.

Christiane started to cry. "Oh Mom, I'm so sad. Jay told me last night he would always be watching over us and looking out for Shelby."

"I know he will, sweetie."

The calls continued in the same vein to my mom, my sister, and, finally, my youngest daughter, Lisanne. The incongruity between what I was telling my family while sitting outside the hospital on a bench in the fading sunshine on what felt like a balmy day in January with temperatures soaring into the mid-fifties struck me.

But now, as the sun dropped behind a row of clouds, I was going back to our house, a widow at age sixty. I didn't know any widows at sixty. I was incredibly young. How could this be happening? I realized I'd never made the drive to our house in this status before, although I'd driven home alone from hospitals plenty of times in the last six months. This was different. Something had changed. I reluctantly got into the car and, for once, was happy to be ensconced in the 5 p.m. traffic. It made the trip so long. I approached our subdivision and found myself driving down our street, pulling into the garage.

A FEAR GREATER THAN DEATH ITSELF

I walked into the house and was immediately drawn to the picture of the angel Jay had purchased for our new house five years before. Something in this picture of a Renaissance angel had "spoken" to him, and he'd envisioned it hanging on the soaring dining room wall with its cathedral ceiling. Now, as I gazed at it, the angel appeared to radiate bright light even though darkness had fallen outside. The angel comforted and ripped me open. Love was in the room. For the first time that day, my emotions took over. I fell on my knees and sobbed before her, with a grief and a heaviness so great I wouldn't have known how to speak of it to anyone. I was singularly alone with a fear greater than death itself. This was the fear of moving forward, moving on, without the presence of my beloved soulmate by my side. I was utterly shaken and abandoned. I recalled the words of C. S. Lewis, written after he lost his wife Joy to cancer, "No one ever told me that grief felt so like fear."[3]

This, I realized, was what it felt like to have your life change in a heartbeat or in a breath. I'd been told not to *fight it*; that fighting a new reality increases the resistance, which makes it worse. But who among us is prepared to have a loved one erased in an instant? How would it be possible for me to let go of the lifeline to him that had accrued in so many heartbeats and so many breaths? And why would I want to? It was counterintuitive to let go of my beloved. What made sense was to hold on to him for as long as I could. To bury my nose in the scent of his clothes, still hanging fresh and crisp in the closet. To hold fast to the routines we'd enjoyed together, the love notes we'd left each other on sticky pads in the mornings, the CD we'd listened to at Thanksgiving, the last time we made love, the movie we watched in bed together, still in the DVD player waiting for the next replay. Yet the next time I'd be in our marital bed alone, never to feel my beloved's warm body next to mine again. And the last thing I'd feel like doing then would be repeating what I just did with him, only this time by myself while feeling the rhythm of my heartbeat, unanswered. No part of me wanted to accept that. I just wanted what I wanted, and that was to have my old life and my beloved back in my arms to have and to hold, just as we'd promised in our wedding vows. Without the *death 'til we part* clause.

I had survived *his* death, but could I survive *my* life? The future lay open to me as some huge, vacant abyss. I still had an abundance of work as a psychologist, but something in my essential identity now seemed lost, my new self unknown. I was no longer a wife. My two daughters had recently left home, so my role as a mother was also greatly diminished. I felt adrift in a large ocean with no borders of land. Who would I be and what would I become?

I realized that most of my energies during the last six months had been spent taking care of Jay, worrying about him and his needs. I'd given precious little thought to this new stage of life for me, left so bereft. Something in me had been dying, too; now I had to figure out what would be reborn.

5

MANIFESTATIONS OF THE SOUL FOLLOWING DEATH

> If you stop and look deeply, you will recognize your beloved manifesting again and again in many forms.[1]
> —Thich Nhat Hanh

Wondering whether the soul exists beyond the body was now an ever-present question, and I couldn't have imagined how soon and unequivocally I'd get an answer.

Jay and I had loved to watch movies together, and one of our favorites was *Ghost*, with Demi Moore and Patrick Swayze. We'd watched *Ghost* at least half a dozen times and always agreed we would contact each other should one of us pass on first. (Our illusionary hope was that we would grow old together and die simultaneously.) So it didn't really come as a huge surprise that I experienced many contacts from Jay after he died, especially in the first few years.

Manifestations of Form

Jay detested funerals. He'd donated his body to medical science and wanted a memorial service instead. I sat on the front row of the church where his father had been the United Methodist minister in Morgantown forty years before, flanked by my daughters on my left, one of Jay's best friends on my immediate right, and Jay's youngest daughter and her husband next to him. It was a long and moving service, with

spectacular, soaring music that another of Jay's best friends had selected and arranged, complete with a eulogy from yet another of Jay's
friends. Many of Jay's clients were there and spoke of the healing they'd
received from their therapeutic work with him. At the end of the service, as the last piece of majestic music was being played, I saw a form
stride down the left aisle of the church to the front of the sanctuary and
just sort of hang there. It had the shape of a person, but without the
definitive features of a physical body. I continued to see this form
around our house after returning from the morning service and on
some occasions thereafter. The night of the service, I woke up at 2 a.m.
and saw Jay's face right in front of me, wearing a huge smile. I knew
what that meant. His memorial service had been pleasing to him in
every way.

There were also many other instances when I simply felt Jay's presence and energies surrounding me. For example, on most nights when I
got into my side of the bed, which was on the right, the left side of the
bed vibrated, much like the sensations experienced when reclining in a
massager chair. Whenever Lisanne, my youngest daughter, came home
to visit me, she would crawl into our bed and lay on Jay's side and feel
the vibrations as well.

Over the years, Jay and I had given each other many cards that we
saved, and for months after his passing, I found solace in looking at
those cards and his handwritten notes. Not too long after his passing, I
discovered one card that had this printed on the inside of it:

Even if you don't see me
Know that I am always here
Jay had added: "*Surrounding you! Love, Jay.*"

That card has been on my bureau ever since. We usually dated our
cards and letters, but this particular one wasn't dated, so I have no idea
how long it was before his cancer diagnosis that I received it. As time
went on, I continued to find other little things I had tucked away,
forgotten, only to bring fresh tears when I came upon them, in remembrance of how much my husband had loved me and how desperate I
was to feel him with me once again.

In my address book, I found a note he'd left one morning while I was
still asleep and he was departing for work. It said:

Sweetheart,

1. *I love you!*
2. *Rusty's on the porch* [our golden retriever]
3. *Door's locked*
4. *It's 8:30 am*

Til the angels close my eyes,
Gunner

We had many nicknames for each other, and Gunner was one of the nicknames I had for him. Rusty had died about ten years before Jay's cancer diagnosis, so I wondered what possessed Jay to sign the note, *"Til the angels close my eyes."* Was there a part of him that knew in some mysterious, unknowing-yet-knowing way that this was going to be his path, his future?

Visitation Dreams

And then there were the dreams! About two weeks after Jay passed, I had my first dream in which he visited me and gave me a message. Apparently, "visitation" dreams from our deceased loved ones are fairly common in cultures all around the world.[2] Geri Grubbs defines visitation dreams as dreams in which a deceased loved one returns in a dream state to provide guidance, reassurance, and/or in some instances, even a warning.[3] Many of my friends and clients who have lost a beloved have shared some of their visitation dreams with me, although not everyone who loses someone precious has such dreams.

Joel Martin and Patricia Romanowski note that while visitation dreams are more common among the widowed and African Americans, there are things you can do to enhance the possibility of having, recognizing, and remembering a visitation dream from a deceased loved one.[4] First, prior to going to sleep, visualize the person and ask for a dream and indicate that you will remember the dream upon awakening. When you have a dream, write it down immediately. I keep a notepad and pen in my nightstand drawer for this purpose. Don't get discouraged if visitation dreams do not come immediately upon engaging in these behaviors. Continue to make requests, use visualization and imagery, and write down ALL dreams to help you remember them and you may be surprised at what occurs in the future.

Carl Jung, who wrote prolifically about the power and meaning of dreams, had his own visitation dream after his wife died in 1963. Jung regarded dreams as something that happens along our path toward wholeness (the word healing means "to make whole"). After his dream about his deceased wife, he believed that these kinds of dreams enabled us to see the deceased as an authentic, whole person rather than as a projection of who we wanted them to be.[5]

Martin and Romanowski, who conducted research on visitation dreams, concluded that there are particular characteristics of these dreams, including the perception that the encounter is very profound, the deceased appears as they did in real life and almost always physically and emotionally healthier, the dream is experienced by the dreamer as a real visit, the dream provides peace and comfort to the griever, and there is usually a simple but meaningful message provided in the dream, the meaning of which is quite apparent.[6] I have had a number of visitation dreams with Jay and as you will read in the following accounts of some of them, all of these characteristics showed up in my dreams!

The Buffalo Dream

Slightly more than two weeks after Jay passed, I had to endure my first Valentine's Day alone. Like our birthdays and our anniversary, Valentine's Day was a special day for us that we celebrated in an intentional way. We planned what we called time away from time to unplug ourselves from the world. Sometimes we went out of town for a romantic overnight; other times we had dinner at home with candlelight, flowers, and music. There were always lots of cards and some gifts we exchanged as well. This first Valentine's Day without Jay I couldn't stop crying. I hadn't gone back to teaching yet and was certainly in active grief mode. But that night I had the first of what some therapists refer to as a "big dream"—a dream that stays with you for the rest of your life because it has a profound effect on you and/or because it represents "stirrings about the unlived potential in your outer life."[7]

I dreamed Jay and I drove out of Morgantown so I could interview for a job that truly fascinated me. Jay was in the role of guide, adviser. I was so excited about the job because it was unlike anything I'd ever done before, until I found out it was located in Buffalo, New York. I said, *"Honey, you know I hate cold weather and snow. I just don't want to move to Buffalo. I don't care how great this opportunity is going to be."* He responded: *"I know this wouldn't be your first choice, but I think it's a good move for you and I know it will work out well eventually."*

When I woke up, I had a strong sense that Jay was being my mentor, letting me know this new life chapter would, over time, develop into something positive, perhaps even fascinating. When my psychologist colleague pointed out that the symbolism of the buffalo in the Native American tradition means protection and abundance, the meaning of the dream was even more intriguing. Later, I discovered some additional information from Ted Andrews's book, *Animal Speak*, which also helped clarify the meaning of the dream. The Lakota were taught that the sign of the white buffalo in particular meant if the right action was connected to the proper prayer, struggling to survive could be avoided, but only if action is allowed to flow easily and not forced.[8]

The fact that I had this dream on my first Valentine's Day without the physical presence of my beloved *was* very comforting to me. Indeed, there is some speculation that visitation dreams help us heal the abandonment we experience after the loss of our beloved. This was not lost on me—my beloved, though gone in the physical form, managed to find a way to show up and still be with me on Valentine's Day—a HUGE blessing for me. Later, as the veil of grief lifted, I realized this big dream was also a message about pursuing potential in my own life, not yet realized at the time of Jay's passing.

Low Spot of Grief

On April 8, about ten weeks after Jay's passing, I descended to a very low place, the lowest spot in my grief journey. I was the sickest I'd been in years. I had a horrible cough and couldn't sleep, so I ended up sleeping upright in the lounge recliner that had always been Jay's chair in our downstairs family room. As his own illness ensued, he'd spent many nights sleeping upright in that chair, too. I had trouble breathing, and it wasn't lost on me that in Chinese medicine, the lungs are the organ of grief. I felt empty, lonely, without purpose. I had a sense of dislocation and disconnection. New routines felt so uncomfortable. I thought many people had "gone away" and weren't checking in with me as much. Eating dinner alone was terribly challenging for me. I wondered why people didn't think of this and invite me over to have dinner with them. I just felt raw. I felt peripheral to everything and everyone. I believed that some of my friends really didn't "get" the depths of my suffering, and I was angry that they still had their spouses when mine was gone. In retrospect, I realized this point in my journey was what Jung calls *"The Dark Night of the Soul"*—a period of spiritual desolation in which there is no awareness of consolation as one's framework for life has collapsed.[9]

The Book of Job Dream

The law of nature states that everything has a frequency vibration, including emotions and thoughts. And everything vibrates at a different level, ranging from a low-frequency vibration for shame, guilt, apathy, and grief, to a high one for love, joy, peace, and enlightenment, and certain frequency vibrations can attract or repel disease.[10] No wonder I developed this illness that took hold of my body and was very hard to shake. The low-frequency vibration of grief had finally caught up with me. On the night when I was the sickest, at my lowest point of all, I had an incredible dream, which I called "The Book of Job" dream.

In this dream, Jay was still alive, but barely. He was clearly very sick and was dying. He said to me, *"I have a message for you—in the Book of Job."* Then my father—who had passed in October, three months before Jay—walked into the room. My dad was older in the dream than he'd been—ninety—when he passed, but he was healthy, not demented as he'd been in the last few years of his life. I said to Jay, *"How can my father be here? Isn't he supposed to be dead?"* Jay replied, *"Well he's here, isn't he?"*

When I woke up, I pondered the meaning of the dream. I searched for information about the messages of the Book of Job, rediscovering that Job was a figure whose faith was severely tested by God in several ways. Job's children were all killed and gone; Job went bankrupt and became quite ill. Essentially, his story is about the meaning of suffering. Job experiences a complete reversal of fortune and when his friends visit, he tells them he can't understand why he's suffering so much. Initially, Job longs for an end to his suffering, perhaps even death. Eventually, his pleas are heard by God and Job learns to trust that his suffering will endure and have meaning. I could relate to that. I DID feel like Job. Why was I suffering? What had I done to deserve this? Why had God abandoned me, too? But like Job, could I, would I find meaning and transformation in the suffering as I endured my grief journey? I assumed when Jay said, "*I have a message for you in the Book of Job,*" it meant I should discover how Job was able to heal his suffering and trust that I would be able to do so, too.

During this three-week illness, I had terrible physical symptoms as well as emotional ones. I felt very particular about what I did and didn't want. I had times of very limited patience, I only wanted certain foods to eat, and I didn't want any light. It occurred to me that I felt like Jay had when his illness became worse. I started to understand how hard it would have been for him to have lived while feeling so physically depleted and limited. I think in that moment I forgave him for dying.

At some level, this dream was a message for me. Both Jay and my father, important male figures in my life, recognized my suffering and wanted me to discover a religious/spiritual message and solution to my suffering through the biblical story of Job. The Dark Night of our Soul is a time of tremendous suffering. It represents a kind of death for ourselves as we experience utter meaninglessness and lack of purpose. Yet it also represents an initiation from one phase of life to another. The other side of The Dark Night of the Soul is a spiritual awakening. In other respects, I feel this was also a dream about Jay. My guess is that he was at a low spot in his journey and was suffering too, missing me and our daughters, his sister, and close friends. It wasn't lost on me that in death, as in life, we were both suffering together! It's been said that when your loved ones show up as sick or dying in a dream, they need our prayers the most.[11]

No Demons Anymore Dream

On June 16, over four months after Jay passed and close to the first wedding anniversary I would spend without him, I woke up from another profound dream I entitled "No Demons Anymore." This wasn't a dream *about* Jay; this was a dream *with* Jay. He came to me and we had a conversation. He hadn't aged and looked the way he had prior to becoming sicker with cancer. He was healthy, but clearly, he had passed on. This wasn't a dream of us in the past; this was a dream of us in the now. He said, "*The best thing about where I am now is that there are no demons here. I'm not haunted by could haves, should haves, or by second-guessing myself or someone else, or by hurting someone else with my words—I'm just happy and peaceful now."* I replied, "It's so helpful to me to hear this. Could we have these visits more often?"

Like Martin and Romanowski found in their research on visitation dreams,[12] Jay appeared physically and emotionally healthy in this dream. And he provided me in this dream a message about *his transformation postdeath*. While some visitation dreams give messages for the survivor, some also contain messages about the journey of the departed and this one did!

In the second part of the dream, we made love for the first time since he'd passed away. He appeared in physical form in this dream and we both were naked and had an intense body-to-body experience without traditional sexual intercourse. I woke up from the dream feeling it had been the most soul-connected, satisfying lovemaking I'd ever experienced. Over the years of our relationship, Jay and I had had a rich sexual connection. Jay used to tell our very close friends that we spent Sundays at "the church of Saint Mattress," and I'd been missing the physical contact with my beloved so strongly—not so much the satisfaction of release, but the soul-to-soul, body-to-body, heart-to-heart contact. This dream showed me that the kind of contact I yearned for still exists even after the soul of someone departs from the body. And again, as other people have discovered in their visitation dreams, I had the sense of having had a real visit with Jay in the dream experience.

Spiritual Rehabilitation Dream

These kinds of dreams have continued intermittently during the last nine years. During the anniversary of Jay's passing each year, I had many dreams in which we are reunited. These dreams speak to our soul connection and at the same time include something about his journey postdeath. Near the first anniversary of his passing, I had a dream in which I felt a surge of electrical energy move through my sleeping body. I woke up from a very powerful dream in which we had been separated but were now together again. We held each other and said how much we'd missed each other. He described to me how he'd gone through what he called a *"spiritual rehabilitation"* process. I felt he was a transformed person in that any woundedness he'd carried here on earth was gone. In this dream, we forgave each other for any lack of kindness on our parts. This dream reminded me of one of my favorite Rumi quotes: "The wound is the place where light enters you." When I awoke from this dream, I felt alive and refreshed and knew beyond a shadow of a doubt that we'd been with each other during the night. It was an indescribable experience except that I can say that the connection between us was more powerful than ever.

Reiki

About four months after Jay's passing, I began doing Reiki sessions with a healer named Christine. Reiki is a Japanese stress-reduction and relaxation approach that's spiritually guided and enhances life-force energy and promotes healing by the practitioner's transmission of energy through the laying on of hands. After my first Reiki session, I experienced the greatest sense of peace I'd felt since Jay had passed. Both Jay and I had been doing cranial sacral work with a Reiki master who, several months prior to Jay's passing, had moved out of state. Cranial sacral therapy, like Reiki, involves laying fully clothed on a table, and having noninvasive touch applied to or near particular parts of the body. Jay's cancer appeared to be in remission during the time he was obtaining cranial sacral work. This wasn't surprising to me since both of these approaches, like acupuncture, are thought to work by removing blocked energy called *chi*, thereby restoring the natural energy flow in the body. I'd found cranial sacral work to be very relaxing and after Marcia moved, I'd missed the comfort of these sessions and decided to give Reiki a try. I enjoyed the Reiki sessions so much that when I had the opportunity to study the approach, I took all three levels of classes, eventually becoming a Reiki Master.

Reiki can be used for any emotional or physical ailment. Ehlers describes potential benefits of Reiki for bereavement as promoting relaxation, improving sleep, assisting with pain management, reducing anxiety and stress, and improving circulation and digestion.[13] In my experience, Reiki lifted the weight of sorrow and helped me find peace, calmness, and clarity.

Close to the first anniversary of his passing, after working with Christine for nine months, Christine got a message from Jay during the Reiki session. Christine said he was still around but not in a visceral way because he had moved to a different level of spiritual development. Jay said to Christine, *"Tell Sherry to enjoy the earthly goods."* With this message, I think Jay was saying, *"Look, I've now been gone a year. You've had a rough and challenging year fraught with sadness, grief, and bereftness. I get it. But now it's year two and YOU are still alive and I want to make sure you get some pleasure and enjoyment from being alive."* I got the message, although clearly, I was still very grief-stricken and pleasure was scant.

Reading from a Psychic Intuitive and Curiosity about an Afterlife

Given the nature of the visitation dreams I'd had with Jay, my interest in the concept of an afterlife simply grew stronger. I became more curious about what happens to the spirit, soul, or consciousness of a person after the physical body dies. I found great wisdom in a book on life after death written by the illustrious Deepak Chopra, whom I'd seen interviewed many times on television.[14] I liked how he described the concept of an afterlife from various religious and spiritual faith traditions. While belief in an afterlife is consistent with Christianity and most other world religions, few religious traditions actively encourage contact between the living and deceased. I was mesmerized by some of Chopra's experiences with death he had growing up in India as well as his description of other grief survivors' visitation dreams with their deceased loved ones. I found comfort in his words that a physical body expresses a particular frequency and that other frequencies that we can't see are "out there" for different planes of existence. His concept of an afterlife was so stunning that I wanted to continue my exploration of what happens after our body dies. When the opportunity came to be a part of a small-group experience with a visiting psychic medium, I grabbed it. Clearly I'm not alone in this search, as many folks consult mediums and psychics in an effort to contact or be contacted by a departed loved one.[15]

And so it was that during the spring of the second year following Jay's passing, I had a reading from an out-of-state psychic intuitive, Doreen, who came to Morgantown to do a group reading for a small number of people. Jay's spirit came through to Doreen during this reading. I'd never met her before and she knew nothing about me or any of the other people in this group of fifteen who'd gathered for readings. She asked me if the person she was seeing was someone who loved life and loved being outdoors. I said yes on both counts. She said, *"He is whistling now."* She said she could feel something restricted in his chest and wondered if he had an illness that was involved in his death. I confirmed that he'd had cancer that had metastasized to the lungs. She asked me if he had helped me through a health challenge of my own and I confirmed that he had. She wondered if I could still feel the *"deep, deep, deep soul connection between us,"* and I said yes! She said, *"He was and still is your protector and is watching over you. He will make sure you're on earth as long as you need to be here but he can't wait until you cross over and join him in the spiritual realm."* She also said, *"He is always in the vehicle with you"*—driving isn't something I enjoy—*"and he loves it when you sing while you drive"*—something I do to ease my uneasiness about driving. *"He wants you to know he loves the new length of your hair now—he wants you to know he loves EVERYTHING about you. He sends you a white rose that symbolizes his abiding love and deep soul connection. He also knows it's late spring and that your favorite season in which you swim all the time with your neighbor is coming up and he's happy about that."* By this point I was sobbing, and many of the group members were also crying from the profound experience of the reading.

Resurrection Dream

In the late summer of the second year following Jay's passing, Senator Ted Kennedy died of a brain tumor. I woke up at 6 a.m. the morning after Senator Kennedy's passing from the following dream: My mother and I were sitting in a row with Jay on my right, even though it was eighteen months after his passing. Then my dad suddenly appeared and sat on my left, in between my mom and me. I remember feeling so happy because clearly my dad had died and yet now he was back and alive, appearing to me as if he'd been "resurrected." I turned to Jay and said with excitement, *"My dad's back and I can actually touch him."* My dad looked his age—ninety—but was happy and peaceful, and in the dream, I did touch him. As in visitation dreams reported by others, my dad appeared healthy, even "reborn." As Grubbs points out, often a resurrection dream suggests a new kind of relationship with the deceased,[16] in this case my dad.

When I woke up, I wondered if this was the mission of people who pass on. That is, to make themselves known and their energies present as some unseen or seen force to those of us still walking here on earth. There are many books about how we can choose a life full of accomplishments, much like Senator Kennedy. But not much attention is given to our mission as souls after we pass out of our physical bodies. I've always wondered, for example, how many angel souls we couldn't see who were around ministering to the thousands of people on 9/11 as they jumped from the burning towers to their certain death.

What's It Like to Die? Dream

Almost two years after his passing, Jay came to me in another dream. He was clearly well and told me he'd moved to another level of spiritual development. I could sense that, not only because he looked so well physically, but also because he seemed healed emotionally. I had the strong sense that all his here-on-earth hurts had been transformed. I asked him two questions in the dream: *"Why did you have to die so early?"* And *"What's it like to die?"* All he said in response was, *"Just wait, it's genius!"*

During the week of the second-year anniversary of his passing, I dreamed I was in a church at an event organized by our friend Joan, and to honor Jay, I asked the people there to sing "Happy Birthday" to him. I said, *"We're going to sing to someone who's not here because science didn't have a solution for his health condition."* So we all sang "Happy Birthday" to Jay! My youngest daughter, Lisanne, interpreted this as a sign of Jay's rebirth and began referring to the day of his passing as a birthday. Stephen Levine, the noted spiritual teacher best known for his work on death and dying, states that "everything in consciousness is constantly dying and being reborn."[17]

Many people I've shared this dream with have found great comfort in the short, simple yet clear message Jay offers in the dream about death: "Just wait: It's genius." This visitation dream, like those reported by many others, contained a short, simple but powerful message and the fact that Jay was physically and emotionally healed in this dream, almost two years after his death, helped my healing immensely.

A Different House Dream

In the spring of that second year, I dreamed I was living in a different house and a different town from Morgantown. The new house was wonderful but needed some work. In this dream, I went away for the weekend, and when I returned, Jay was in the new house and had completed the work. It was now beautiful in all respects. I wondered about the meaning of being in a different house in another location because I was constantly debating about my purpose in life and whether I should stay in Morgantown and continue my work there as a psychologist or leap somewhere else. I kept going back and forth because I loved my teaching and my work with clients, but I also felt something pulling me away. I also recognized that this dream was not only about an external move away, but also about an internal shift. Houses, in dreams, are symbolic of the self. One of my most treasured books Jay ever gave me is called *House as a Mirror of Self*.[18] Some part of me had died with Jay and now something was being reborn, but still needing growth.

During the fourth year after Jay's death, I found a small beach cottage south of Annapolis, moved, and officially became a resident of the state of Maryland, having lived in West Virginia for the better part of my adult life. It's perhaps significant that I found my cottage four years after Jay's death, as the number four represents wisdom, equilibrium, and birth.[19]

I felt concerned about how Jay would perceive my move and whether I would still have the same kind of metaphysical contact with him after moving to my new cottage. I've been in my Starfish cottage for six years now, and while the dreams of Jay are more infrequent, he still does appear to me periodically at night.

Rumi says:

In your light I learn how to love,
In your beauty, how to make poems.
You dance inside my chest, where no one sees you, but sometimes I do, and that sight becomes this art.[20]

Jay was still dancing inside my chest after my move to Maryland.

Starfish Cottage Dreams

My first dream about Jay following the move occurred on the fourth anniversary of his passing, after I'd lived in my new location for five months. In the dream, I'd been out running errands and when I came back inside the cottage, I found Jay in the master bedroom assembling a new bed for the two of us! I flew into his arms and said, *"Honey, I haven't seen you for so long."* He was clearly four or five years older in this dream but was in great health. I wasn't surprised by this dream; Jay loved to assemble and make things. Our bed was always our special place, not just because of great sex but also because we experienced so much comfort in each other's physical presence.

After living in the cottage for a year, I dreamed again I'd moved to the cottage, clearly alone, without Jay. Jay's daughter Laura was in the dream and I said, *"Laura, I can't understand why Jay is gone from my life and I'm here alone."*

I ended up writing Jay a letter, telling him how much I missed him and asking him where he was and if he was okay. The next thing I knew in the dream, I was standing outside on my back deck with the dog I'd rescued after Jay's passing, my golden retriever Abbey. Jay appeared in the corner of the backyard. He looked just as he had five years ago, but healthy and happy. Abbey ran to him and jumped up on him and yelped for joy. It was as if they knew each other. Jay and I didn't speak in this dream, but we looked at each other, and our connection was unbroken and as strong as ever. That night, I felt the vibrations that occurred previously once more in my bed. And the next morning, Abbey, who never stirred off her bed in the living room until I was out there myself, was up and prancing around as if she was playing with someone!

It's significant to me that in this third dream about my new cottage, unlike the first two, I was now alone, without Jay, in the house. And when Jay did appear in the dream, he showed up in a corner of the backyard, the boundary between my cottage and the house behind me. Clearly his journey postdeath was taking him farther away from me, and probably my journey was pulling me away from him. As Grubbs suggests, this is really by necessity. She indicates there's a fine line between letting go of a loved one too soon and holding on too long.[21]

On New Year's Eve, almost five years after Jay's passing, I woke up in the middle of the night and felt him next to me in bed with his arms embracing me. I know for certain Jay was next to me in the bed because kinesthetically I could actually feel the warmth of his embrace. I asked him, *"If you can come tonight, why can't you be here every night like this?"* He didn't answer this question directly but said, *"I was told I should not die since I was so well loved but the sea carried me away anyway."*

On the surface, the meaning of this dream seemed more obtuse. However, in a dream, the sea often represents spiritual awakening. Many of these bigger dreams I've had about Jay were not only messages from him for me and my path, but also messages about the path he was on after passing away. To me, this dream meant that even though Jay recognized the depth of everyone's love for him, each of us must follow our own spiritual path and passing away when he did was part of his path. Pierre Teilhard de Chardin, the French Jesuit priest who was also a mystic, wrote during the year of his own death: *"We are not human beings having a spiritual experience; we are spiritual beings having a human experience."* [22] No matter how much we're loved here on earth, no one can prevent us from being on the spiritual journey each of us is destined to take. Grubbs indicates that "it is meant for the departed to go forward in his or her soul's journey rather than cling to or feel responsible for your emotional work here on Earth." [23] This dream indicated I was still longing for Jay, yet it was time for me to start letting go.

Meaning of the Dreams

Eventually, these dreams helped me accept that Jay's death, though untimely for me, was part of his spiritual journey. It occurred to me that even though he was so cherished by me, his family, and his clients, perhaps dying when he did was part of his soul's path, and he needed to move on in order to grow, develop, and have a different mission—at one point, I had a dream that after he passed away, he was serving the homeless, and another intuitive reader told me he was working with young people after they died. I suffered less about these questions after reading a book written by the Vietnamese Buddhist Zen master and peace activist Thich Nhat Hanh: *Fear: Essential Wisdom for Getting Through the Storm.* In it, he writes about releasing fears of the future by focusing on remembrances that include growing old, having ill health, dying, and carrying the results of our acts with us. [24]

This last remembrance speaks to the concept of karma; that when we die, what continues are our thoughts, words, and actions, wholesome and unwholesome. These remembrances helped me understand that each of us is on a spiritual path full of karmic acts that no one else in our life, no matter how much they care about us, can do or undo.

However, from the instant Jay was diagnosed with cancer, I'd been obsessed with trying to save him; in retrospect, I realized the inflation in my behavior. I pulled out all the stops: we bought a high-powered juicer and he had daily organic vegetable juice drinks complete with kale and broccoli, each containing anticarcinogenic compounds; I tried to admonish him about his sugar habit because too much sugar weakens the immune system and creates inflammation in the body; I sent him to my acupuncturist, and although that wasn't a good fit for him, he did very good work with a seasoned cranial sacral body worker. And I tried to get him to meditate because we know mediation calms the agitated monkey mind and a calm mind leads to neurochemical changes in the brain and the body that, in turn, strengthen the immune system.

As a psychologist specializing in wellness and lifestyle issues, I was concerned about the mind-body link in the development of illness because one's state of mind and emotional health impact the body and influence the state of cell growth.[25] In some ways, I did feel as if Jay was in a state of spiritual stagnation prior to his cancer diagnosis. He was working very hard at taking care of his clients but had neglected his own well-being except for his regular visits to the gym. His parents had both died in the five years prior to his diagnosis, and I felt as if he'd stuffed his feelings about these losses. I'd say, "Honey, how are you feeling about your dad's death?" or "Do you think you've processed the fact your mom died so suddenly?" and he'd say, "I don't know." But at one point after his parents both were gone, he said spontaneously, "I'm an orphan now." His unprocessed grief led me to recall the statement made by Judy Tatelbaum: "Grief unexpressed is like a powder keg waiting to be ignited."[26]

And as wonderful as Jay was, he did, *as we all do*, have a shadow side to him that was probably only apparent to me. At times, I think he felt conflicted about his success with his clients, either feeling he wasn't successful enough or feeling his success had surpassed his father's, which somehow was wrong. In addition, he could be quite reactive to situations and people and get emotionally stirred up in a short amount of time, during which high levels of the stress hormone cortisol almost certainly flooded his body. These dreams, however, showed me that the mind-body issues he'd experienced on earth were being healed in the continuation of his spiritual journey after he passed away.

While my dreams about Jay became less frequent, during the week of the sixth anniversary of his passing, this time on vacation at Sanibel Island, Florida, I had many dreams about him. On January 28, the day of his passing, I woke up shortly after going to sleep with a surge of electrical energy jolting through my body. In addition to the vibrations in the bed, there have been times when I've literally been jolted awake in the night or during a dream. It's not an unpleasant feeling, but rather one of awakening, something akin to extremely high vibrational energies. Later in the night, I woke up again from a very powerful dream in which Jay had visited and we made love. In healthy healing of grief, visitation dreams do fade away, but often reappear at a time of crisis or significance such as the anniversary date of a passing.

There's no doubt that these visitation dreams helped heal my bereftness and guide me toward wholeness. The dreams were instructive about my healing and spiritual awakening (as well as Jay's journey postdeath). In some therapeutic traditions, dreams represent inner parts of ourselves. Would I be the person I am today if I hadn't had the experience of losing my beloved? I don't think so. Not by choice, but by necessity, in coping with all these deaths, I've had to grow up. Much like Job in the Bible, and much like finding a fascinating new job but not wanting to suffer for it in cold, snowy Buffalo, I resisted change and didn't like what the suffering was doing to me.

But that has shifted. I've learned that life is change and everything and everyone all around us are constantly reflecting states of impermanence. Change is growth and lack of change is stagnation. While the suffering was challenging for me, it made me much more attuned to the suffering of others. My grief journey has had a tremendously positive impact on my work. About nine months after Jay passed, I realized I was doing some of the best teaching and therapy of my career. There were many days when I had the strong sense I was channeling Jay, an extremely gifted therapist, in my own work. I'd always been a sensitive and caring instructor and practitioner, but now I had even more compassion and a better understanding of what people were up against in their respective life journeys, and this quality shone through much like the brilliance of snow crystals glistening in the bright, midday sun.

One of the areas in which the most growth has occurred for me had to do with what therapists call *individuation*, meaning the act of differentiating yourself from another. The Jungians believe that individuation is often brought on by a catastrophic event or earth-shaking loss that challenges everything you believe and leaves you completely altered. Jay and I *were* joined at the hip. It was hard to imagine myself without him because we were so connected to each other and we did everything together. I didn't have much of a life of my own apart from the coupleship. I think in part this was the natural result of the fact that this was a remarriage for both of us. We were very intentional about keeping our emotional connection strong. In addition, my contribution to this situation was probably some long-standing abandonment anxiety. But after Jay passed away, my abandonment anxieties healed. After all, the worst possible abandonment had occurred and I'd survived it.

I've read many books since Jay's passing that have been extremely helpful to me. But none of them elucidated my growing philosophy about life after death more clearly than the one I mentioned earlier by Thich Nhat Hanh, in which he described his journey with grief for over a year following his mother's death, until one night he had this dream about her.[27] He saw himself sitting with her having a wonderful talk, and she was young and beautiful and vibrant and, he said, it was as if his mother had never died. Following that dream, he wrote that he had a very strong feeling that his mother was still with him, and he hadn't lost her after all!

Thich Nhat Hanh acknowledged that suffering occurs with deep loss, but also that there is really no-birth, no-death, just manifestation, followed by the cessation of manifestation in order to have another manifestation. I realized how fortunate I'd been to be present to and mindful of the many manifestations of Jay—and also my dad—in the years following his passing. And I was reminded of Thich Nhat Hanh's writings once again after I lost my mother, who passed away three years almost to the exact day after Jay passed, in the cold dark days of the first month of the year.

Manifestations of My Mother's Spirit

After flying out to Illinois, where she passed, and visiting her designated funeral home to make service arrangements, I returned to the retirement facility where my mom had been living. It was late afternoon and bitterly cold, but the sky was a cornflower blue with no clouds in sight, and the sun was shining robustly. As I approached the door of the assisted-living unit, my attention was drawn to the left, where I noticed four large bushes directly outside the front windows of my mother's apartment. It was the dead of winter, mid-January, with temperatures hovering in the teens, yet the bushes were teeming with robins. Throngs of robins. I called my brother-in-law's attention to this and after I went inside, the assisted-living staff viewed the spectacle at the window. They were as astounded as I was. None of us had ever noticed robins in mid-January in this climate. But robins were very special to my mother. She hated winter and was always on the lookout for the sign of that first robin. When she saw it, she felt hope. I felt these robins were manifestations of my mother's soul. Again, as with Jay, I would find many other manifestations of my mother following her passing. And once again, I would be reminded of the abiding presence of her love and devotion, despite the absence of her physical body.

I don't fear death now as I did. I believe we have connections post-death with those who were closest to us and who love us the most, even though I recognize that not everyone will experience their loved one's passing in the ways I have. I know for an absolute certainty that after I go, I'll be in the energy fields of my loved ones and that they will feel manifestations of my soul in their lives as, without my physical body, I continue to vibrate my now daily intention, *only love*.

It's often said that the survivors of the deceased person have more of a struggle than the one who passes away. In the last month of his life, while my bereftness was kicking in, Jay assured me I would be okay. I found such reassurance really difficult to accept. In fact, I thought to myself—but didn't share with him—that he really didn't know what he was talking about! It would be many months before I could even begin to agree with his assertion.

6

STARTING OVER AND POSTTRAUMATIC GROWTH

We must be willing to get rid of the life we've planned so as to have the life that is waiting for us. [1]
—Joseph Campbell

After Jay's passing, I struggled to make a life. For several years, I didn't consider doing anything new. Jay's death was so fresh that I wanted to remain in familiar surroundings and do what I'd done for the last thirty-five years: work at the university, teach, see clients, hang out with neighbors, and run into people I knew at the grocery store. Predictable routines and well-known people helped me cope with the anxiety of being alone.

Social Support Following Loss

Social support following a loss or other traumatic event is essential in the healing process. We know this from studying various types of trauma survivors, from terrorism to natural disasters. Close relationships tend to buffer us from the stress of loss and also foster resilience. We have to find ways to compensate for the loss of companionship we endured and typically we accomplish this through finding new connections and substitutions. [2] Supportive help tends to diminish at the end of the anniversary year. While the first year is daunting, the second year, and even the third one, can be more challenging because the finality of the loss or the trauma sets in. Loss of social support during these successive years can make survivors feel even lonelier, perhaps even re-traumatized.

I know this from research and from survivors of loss I've counseled, as well as my own experience. I was inundated with social and emotional support from friends and family for the first year after Jay died. Initially, when I felt like crawling in a hole, the level of support was almost too great to bear. However, by the third year, I felt particularly alone, with only one other widow friend in Morgantown. Renata had lost both her husband and brother during the same time I lost my father and Jay. In addition, Renata was a fellow academic, a strong feminist, and an astute, open, and witty person.

We were navigating new territory, but in sharing our triumphs and failures, we used each other as role models to create growth and forge new paths. While generalized social support is useful in healing from grief and trauma, particular social support from those who've experienced something similar is even better. Renata and I dined together frequently and also phoned each other, often for comfort. As distressed as we both felt, we almost always laughed.

Yet I still felt out of place as a widowed woman in a small town dominated by couples and families. When I went to social events, often I was the only woman at the event of that status, and the conversation was dominated by events and interactions with spouses.

At a typical event, the conversation would go like this:

"Tom and I are going to go skiing during the holidays."

"Oh, how wonderful. Jerry and I are staying home, but we're heading to Florida for several months after the first of the year."

"Well, you guys are lucky. I wanted to go somewhere to get out of the cold, but Timothy nixed that idea. He wants to save money to put in a pool for the summer."

While I was fortunate to have long-term friendships with several couples who were no strangers to loss, I felt as if other coupled friends didn't understand the magnitude of my experience. For example, one of my partnered friends described an older couple she knew with various health challenges: "Their relationship has kept each other alive all these years." Perhaps that's true, but it seemed like an insensitive comment to make to someone like me, whose spouse had recently died and was now single. There are many times when it's so easy to make an offhand, careless remark. We forget about people who just lost a parent or a child on Mother's Day or Father's Day and are actively grieving and not celebrating. Being in a single-status minority group eventually propelled me to think seriously about moving to a different geographical location. And for newly single people who may have an additional minority group affiliation such as sexual orientation, race, and ethnicity, finding adequate social support following loss can be even more daunting, especially in particular geographical areas.

An Urge to Change

Ambivalent, I went back and forth weighing the pros and cons of moving. I was prodded along by changes in the department in which I had been teaching for many years. At the same time, my partner in private practice moved out of state, leaving me to find an alternate place to practice. When I left on trips, I felt reluctant to return to Morgantown. In contrast, when I went to Annapolis to visit my youngest daughter, I felt engaged, vibrant, and noticed a plethora of single women in yoga classes and restaurants. The universe seemed to be giving me gentle nudges that said *go* despite my familiar surroundings. As a psychologist I was acutely aware of the science behind how people make changes and I didn't want to stay stuck in contemplating change as many people do for years.[3] During this third year, my ninety-three-year-old mother's health declined. She died a few days before the fourth anniversary of Jay's passing. With both my parents gone, I felt an impetus to be in closer proximity to my daughters. I was acutely aware I was living in a town without any blood relatives.

By year four of Jay's passing, I was a stronger person. Having to do many things alone gave me courage. The fears and anxieties I'd experienced after Jay's passing had abated. I wanted close connections with my daughters and I needed nourishing friendships with other single women. I craved more creative endeavors. I desired meaningful volunteer work to do. I preferred ties to an area with a strong sense of community. I also wished for closer access to a major airport for easier and more affordable travel. I longed to live in an area with less rain, less snow, more sunshine. And while I loved the mountains of West Virginia, my landlocked inner mermaid yearned to live near a tidal body of salt water because I loved to sail and kayak. I also knew that proximity to

water decreases stress hormones (cortisol) and increases feel-good
chemicals in the brain (dopamine, serotonin, and oxytocin), an effect
recently dubbed the *blue mind*.[4]

Around this time, I met a Vedic astrologer, Richard, from Asheville,
North Carolina. Vedic astrology is based on an ancient Indian method
that uses the constellations to interpret and predict events based on
someone's time and place of birth. To assist in my decision-making, I
contracted with him to do a birth-chart reading and was encouraged
that his reading of the recent and future events in my life coincided
with my visualizations of a divergent direction. Specifically, he mentioned the development of a creative writing endeavor and meaningful
volunteer work.

As a follow-up, I provided Richard with seven potential locations for
a geographic move, including Morgantown as well as Pittsburgh, Char-
lottesville, Sarasota, Wilmington, Chapel Hill, and Annapolis. He gen-
erated a location analysis report for topics such as housing, relationships, finances, career, health, spirituality, and so on. The latter three
locations seemed the most promising for my well-being. Given the
proximity of Annapolis to my youngest daughter, and the ease of getting
from there to my eldest daughter in Pittsburgh, I decided to relocate to
that area. I mentioned to several friends in Morgantown that I was
manifesting a life in a small cottage in a beach community.

I explored real estate in the Annapolis area online every month. It
was discouraging; smaller affordable housing in the area was limited. At
the end of May, a month during which we had only two days of sunshine in Morgantown, I discovered a small renovated cottage for sale in
a beach community seven miles south of Annapolis. The community
itself was at the end of a peninsula and had its own beautiful private
beach with a nature preserve, a marina, and a kayak launch. The cottage
was situated a half block from a lovely cove where sailboat moorings
dotted the water. I called my daughter that day and asked her to take a
look at the interior of the cottage. She called back after her tour.

"Mom," she exclaimed, "this cottage has your name written all over
it."

I went to Annapolis the next day. I was serious enough to make the
trek to Maryland, but it wasn't until I drove up in front of the cottage
that I just knew. There was something about the way the red and yellow
rosebushes encircling the front yard emitted their fragrance when I got

out of the car, calling up the rose garden I had at my Morgantown house. And how the stature of the enormous oak trees surrounding the cottage made me feel safe and protected, as if their wisdom from living tall all these years might somehow be transmuted onto me in this dwelling. But when I stepped inside the cottage, the simple loveliness of it took my breath away. I'd expected it to be small and somewhat simple but hadn't anticipated the vibrancy of the red, blue, and yellow color palette or the sleekness of the cherry kitchen cabinets and granite counters, or the sheen from the beautiful mahogany wood floors throughout. My eyes turned upward to the cathedral ceiling in the living room, where a large decorative sailboat and duck decoy perched on a loft shelf. At the other end of the living room, I took in a porthole window where I could see almost nothing other than the sun dappling through the green leaves of the oak trees outside. I felt enveloped by the house and knew I belonged to it and the house belonged to me, as if we were one. I made an immediate offer on the cottage and owned it by that evening. I called my Pittsburgh daughter, Christiane, to give her the news.

"Mom," she cried. "How exciting! But you don't usually make decisions this quickly."

She was right. Decision-making is intentional and deliberate for me. On this one, I trusted my gut, and my gut said, *Do it and do it now!* Fortunately, the Morgantown real estate market was strong and my house there sold quickly. My Reiki worker said, "Wow! You sure are letting go of a lot at once."

She was right, but I could feel nothing but excitement mounting at the impending changes in my life and the rapidity with which they were occurring.

Postttraumatic Growth (PTG)

Letting go of the old and embracing the new is a sign of transformation of the traumatic event from posttraumatic stress to posttraumatic growth, or PTG. I'm fascinated with PTG because of how and whether people can change and make sense of tragedy. But the bigger reason is because it helps explain my story as a grief survivor, too. Starting over for me meant growth and change!

"Posttraumatic growth," a term coined in the 1990s by psychologists Richard Tedeschi and Lawrence Calhoun, refers to change experienced as a result of adversity.[5] PTG isn't a return to life as it was *before* the trauma. It represents a shift in the way one views the world. One of the best predictors of PTG is an attitude of *acceptance coping*—accepting what one wishes could be changed but can't. Stephen Joseph has described six signposts that facilitate PTG in the acronym THRIVE: Take stock, Harvest hope, Reauthor, Identify change, Value change, and Experience change in action.[6]

PTG is represented by changes in several domains, notably *in a sense of self*—"I'm not who I was before this happened to me," *in relationships with others*—"I'm choosing different persons to be connected with now," and *in a philosophy of life*—"I have different priorities."[7] Perhaps a single word description that best fits what PTG is would be an *awakening*. Your perspective shifts in PTG in particular ways which you could never have imagined prior to the loss or adverse event you endured.

The term "PTG" is new enough in the psychological literature that misconceptions of what it means abound. It shouldn't be equated with simply thinking positively about one's loss. And while it can lead to resilience, it isn't synonymous with it. It's not something that occurs from the loss event itself. Instead, PTG is a result of one's struggle to cope with and make meaning from the event. The development of PTG can be a result of a single or multiple losses or traumas and is often impacted in significant ways by our cultural reference groups and our culturally based core values and beliefs, including those that have to do with religion and spirituality. When achieved, it's generally stable over time. And it's such a relatively new phenomenon that clinicians like myself, while relying on some general helping skills like active listening, need additional training in the processes that are identified as being critical to facilitating PTG in client populations. Tedeschi has published a self-help workbook that provides step-by-step guidelines for ways to promote PTG.[8]

In writing about PTG, Joseph uses the analogy of a valuable vase that's dropped and smashes into a thousand pieces.[9] Trauma is like that treasured broken vase, with life patterns and identities often shattered beyond recognition. Trying to put the pieces of one's life back together like the vase was before it was dropped is unlikely to result in PTG and more likely to mean that life continues to feel fractured. Trying to find something new out of the brokenness can result in PTG. Of course the vase is still broken, so even with PTG, feelings of distress may still exist.

PTG doesn't mean everything is rosy all the time. It's not the same as happiness. Since PTG involves living life at a deeper level, often as a result of the moral depth produced by suffering, periodic reminders of what's been lost compared to what's been gained seem important.[10] PTG typically doesn't occur early in the grief process; some degree of equilibrium needs to be attained first. PTG also is facilitated by social environments in which growth is allowed, perhaps even encouraged. And when survivors don't have to engage in emotional constipation, but instead have the freedom to tell and retell their story about the loss or trauma to caring companions and listeners, the potential for growth is even greater. The noted psychologist Donald Meichenbaum believes that stories are the pathway by which trauma survivors develop sufficient positive coping to achieve growth.[11]

Any event that has a *seismic impact* on one's assumptive world constitutes what Calhoun and Tedeschi construe as a traumatic event. And it's worth noting in these turbulent global times that traumatic events may occur within a family, a community, or a country. Disruptions in functioning occur within a group, yet possibilities of growth also exist within a group as well. As Calhoun and Tedeschi conclude, "Entire societies may be transformed as well as individuals, as social movements and political change can result from catastrophe."[12] Hopeful words as we struggle to make meaning of terrorist attacks, war, climate change catastrophes, and unpredictable times!

PTG also doesn't imply, however, that suffering loss or experiencing trauma is good or desirable. Most people I know would never *choose* to have trauma occur in order to grow! No trauma survivor wants to hear insensitive mantras like "This will make you a better person," or "Look for the silver lining," or—as Kate Bower suggests in her beautiful memoir—"This is happening for a reason."[13] And not everyone who experiences loss or trauma grows from it.[14] A loss involving the sudden and unpredictable death of a loved one constitutes a particular type of traumatic loss. This kind of traumatic loss occurs without any warning and often involves violence and accidents. PTG may be less likely in this kind of loss, especially until after the survivors can build sufficient resources, process the traumatic event, and mourn the loss.[15]

Women report PTG more frequently than men, and those who experience a moderate amount of loss or trauma are more likely to move toward PTG than those who suffer a small or huge trauma. PTG is the positive axis of PTSD or Posttraumatic Stress Disorder. In fact, trauma survivors *with* PTSD exhibited more posttraumatic growth than those trauma survivors who didn't develop PTSD.[16] As Joseph points out, "posttraumatic stress seems to be the engine that drives psychological growth following adversity."[17] While posttraumatic stress and growth exist simultaneously, generally when the growth expands, the stress diminishes.

Persons who are more open to experience and score higher in extraversion also seem more likely to grow in significant ways after traumatic loss.[18] And age may be another factor in who moves toward growth or not after traumatic loss. Younger age, better health, and greater social networks are associated with better adaptation following spousal loss.[19]

When my dad died three months before Jay, my mom was ninety. Dad had suffered dementia for eight or nine years, yet my mom couldn't experience any relief from his absence. She kept saying on the phone, "Sherry, I miss Daddy so much," in between sobs. At her advanced age, moving forward in a new direction seemed impossible. I was often sobbing with her, but I was also mindful of my two young-adult daughters who needed me to model a way forward to heal. I also was convinced Jay wouldn't want me suffering unduly as a result of his passing. These two factors alone pushed me toward growth even on the worst of days. Little did I know moving day would be one of those.

7

TURBULENCE AND CHANGE

Turbulence is life force. It is opportunity. Let's love turbulence and use it for change.
—Ramsey Clark (unsourced)

The night before the movers came, I heard a crash. I tiptoed from my first-floor bedroom to the living room and, turning on a light, saw the handcrafted green pottery pineapple Jay and I had hung next to our front door smashed to smithereens. Some unseen force or presence had brought it down. Was it an omen? A warning? Or simply a symbol that my old life with Jay in this house we'd built together was coming to a screeching halt?

In retrospect, I've decided it was a warning. The day the movers came and my daughter and I loaded my car and drove to Maryland was also the day Hurricane Irene was moving up the coast. By the time we reached my daughter's house, in a neighborhood close to my new cottage, the sky was eerily bright and the wind extremely calm. Still, the forecast was so unsettling, I decided to spend the night at her house. During the night, the wind battered against the roof of her house and the pouring rain sounded like shards of glass hitting the windowpanes. When we got up the next morning, the sun was gleaming and the sky was a cerulean blue. I was about to forget the whole incident when I received a phone call from the woman who resided behind my cottage.

"Hi, Sherry, this is Teresa, your new neighbor who lives behind you. I thought you were due to move in this weekend and I wanted to let you know that your side neighbor's tree fell down during the night, across your fence, and into your backyard. Unfortunately, it brought down a live power line with it."

My heart tumbled to my feet.

I jumped into the car and drove to the cottage. Although it was only a few miles away from my daughter's house, it took me half an hour to get there. There was a steady stream of walkers, bikers, and cars heading up the two-lane road on the peninsula to the one gas station that was open with coffee, water, and basic supplies like toilet paper.

A Backyard Explosion

When I peered gingerly into my backyard, it looked as if a bomb had exploded. The side fence was completely down, the yard was full of debris, and the trunk of the tree rested on the steps to the deck leading to the dining room. The downed power line was not only on the ground; it was actually pulled out of the roof. The scene reminded me of a scarred landscape I'd witnessed as a child after a tornado struck. It was a Sunday and not only were agencies closed, but most places also had lost power. Tears welled in my eyes and began to trickle down my face. I could feel my body start to shake. I could hardly breathe and my heart was beating so loud it sounded like a train pounding down the tracks.

I made my first of many natural-disaster phone calls to my new Maryland insurance agent, who was the epitome of customer service. Being a fellow West Virginian, she even invited me to stay at her home until my power was restored. She personally filed a claim for me after I described the nature of the damage. That was the easy part.

The Meaning of Shelter

Dealing with the neighbors whose tree had fallen into my yard was much more difficult. They were renting the house from an investment company and seemed unable to give me any information about their landlord. They were also quite unimpressed with my situation.

"You still have shelter in the house, don't you?" the man asked.

"Well, yes, but I have no air conditioning or water without power, and there's a live wire down in my side yard," I replied.

"Well, yes, but we all still have shelter," he repeated.

Clearly his definition of shelter didn't coincide with my privileged view. I'd always equated shelter with refuge and protection from the elements. Now I felt vulnerable and exposed. When another neighbor explained that this man, the father of four, had lost his job and his house before finding this rental, I was better able to appreciate his perspective on the myriad of meanings about shelter.

A West Virginia Connection

Sitting in traffic while trying to get back to my daughter's house, my luck shifted. A pickup truck with tree-grinding and removal equipment stopped next to me. With the windows down and stopped traffic, I was able to query him about whether they dealt with downed trees. I discovered that this was their specialty, they were available—after securing coffee—and they were from West Virginia. I smiled for the first time that day, feeling the knot in my stomach releasing a bit. Surely I'd built up good karma in West Virginia; these connections were saviors and rescuers that day.

True to their word, they were at the cottage within the hour and within several hours after that the backyard had been cleared.

Bureaucracy and Regulations

The next day, I found out why Maryland is appropriately described—at least compared to West Virginia—as *an overregulated state*. I was quickly introduced to the bureaucracies of both the power company that serviced my utilities and the county office that inspected and provided work permits. I discovered that repair and restoration of power was likely to be a lengthy process. In the end, it was almost a month before my house had power due, in part, to hurricane damage everywhere, and I'd completely overstayed my welcome with my daughter and her fiancé.

Chaos

Turbulent and chaotic: not the way I'd expected my move to be. My mind kept going back to the smashed pineapple. I started second-guessing my decision to move. I wanted nothing more than to be settled in my cottage, but the universe seemed to be thrusting me in a different direction! Although I felt unraveled, I was sustained by the kindness of many new neighbors and by the efforts of my West Virginia friends to stay in touch with me during my transition. I described my plight to Linda, owner of a healing-arts studio in Morgantown, and one of my wisest women friends.

"That turbulence really isn't a bad thing," she suggested. "When there is that level of turbulence the old energies are cleared, making space for new things to emerge."

What, I wondered, *will come next* as I recalled the words from a note written by my sister, "First light births a new day, presents new challenges: Open your mind to them."[1]

Utopia

Initially, the idea of new challenges was not something I was thinking about once I moved into my cottage and the turbulent energy settled. For a few months after the move I was in utopia. I kept pinching myself to make sure I really lived here. I undertook many projects around the cottage to make its outer manifestation consistent with my internal vision. I replaced the gravel drive with sandstone-hued pavers to match the cedar shake exterior. I also installed a custom mailbox complete with a sailboat cutout, signifying my knowledge that I lived in the sailing capital of the country. The hurricane had proved to be an unexpected gift. Because the neighbors' tree had taken out a large portion of the chain-link fence, I used my damages check to install a white privacy fence. The brightness of the fence, paired with professional landscaping and fieldstone pavers, turned my backyard into an oasis. A St. Francis statue and mermaids reigned over the garden. When I stepped out on my repaired deck, my eyes brightened as I inhaled the slightly salty air coming off a stiff breeze from the nearby Chesapeake Bay and watched an osprey circling overhead.

Most of the furniture in my large house I'd sold to purchase others better-scaled to my dollhouse beach cottage. I'd brought gifts from Jay to grace the walls, including a discarded mirror he'd turned into a beautiful object made from oyster shells, as well as several special anniversary cards he'd matted and framed. A Valentine heart made of small shells he'd constructed one Valentine's Day and a wreath he'd fabricated from our grapevine with shells he'd collected from our beach trips also adorned the walls. The wedding present of original art with an embracing couple hung over my bed. In every room, Jay's stamp was unmistakable! I was aware of engaging in what the grief literature calls *continuing bonds*; practices that grief survivors do to remain connected to their loved one to ease transitions.[2]

The first week here I joined a gym and attended a yoga-for-women class as well as doing my usual cardio and strength training. The yoga class was so popular, there was hardly room to spread out. But I met some fascinating women, including two who invited me to their church. I started going there right away. I loved the friendliness of the church as well as its historic brick building, surrounded by verdant boxwoods and a cemetery with tombstones so ancient the lettering had faded. An after-church social hour enabled me to connect with people. Sundays were lonelier days for me, especially if my daughter was working. Showing up at church and simply being in the presence of other people was reassuring.

I savored the number of warm, sunny days into the New Year walking on the beach. My sea glass collection began. After a few months, many pieces of it decorated my cottage like pieces of ribbon candy. I hadn't made any friends yet, but former colleagues and students lived in the area and I was able to get together with them occasionally. My daughter had enough time off work that we could do many things together, too.

Loneliness and Homesickness

But in late January, coinciding with the anniversary of Jay's passing, I encountered a rough patch. I'd lived here four months and it finally sunk in that this was real. I wasn't on some extended vacation, destined to go back to familiar territory in West Virginia. I missed my friends in Morgantown and longed for friends here. My friend Renata assuaged my nerves by reminding me of her friends who'd moved away and were ready to move back within that first year due to bouts of loneliness.

"I'm sure you remember Lenora, who moved to Arizona after she retired. She almost moved back after the first year because she hadn't made any friends. But she hung in there, and in the second year, things really shifted for her and she's so happy she stayed."

I've since read some research that suggests a primary factor in feeling good about a place is the duration of time we spend there.[3] It takes three to five years after moving to a new place to really become attached to it in a way that makes us feel at home there and enhances our well-being.[4] Who knew? I just assumed because I loved Annapolis it would be a matter of minutes before it felt like home!

Forming New Assumptions

I took Renata's words to heart. According to attachment theory, grief emerges because we no longer have the support system we've become accustomed to in our lives. Like children separated from their mothers, as adults we search for the beloved, now physically lost to us. Meghan O'Rourke, writing in *The New Yorker* about grief, suggests that in the absence of the departed person, we generate a new assumptive world after the former one was refuted by death.[5] The assumptive world concept, first described by C. Murray Parkes, refers to whatever belief system we hold that provides stability and security to our lives. Loss shatters these beliefs and panic and disorientation can ensue.[6]

This principle holds true for any loss—not only of a person, but of a job, a house, a relationship, or any loss of status. Once loss shatters life as we know it, we must begin anew because our familiar bearings are gone. Healing occurs gradually as we form new assumptions in our worldview, and this could be the most critical task of mourning.

Seeking Connections

I realized I was gradually building a new worldview and identity here, but it involved completely starting over. I tried to practice what I preached to clients about the importance of developing social networks and taking action. I knew the quantity of social connections is an important component of health and well-being, especially without a formal employment setting. Mindful that I'd moved here without a job or school-aged children, I recognized intentionality was necessary to acquire new social networks. I developed a general strategy with four components: (1) to stay open to any new options, (2) to say yes to anything (unless it was illegal or dangerous!), (3) to introduce myself liberally to everyone, and (4) to commit to exploration. Melody Warnick also provides a helpful guidebook for learning to love and enjoy a new environment. She suggests such activities as walking more, buying local, getting to know neighbors, exploring nature, volunteering, and getting involved in community and political affairs.[7]

I started talking to everyone I met, indicating I was new to the area. At my bank, the manager recruited me to volunteer on the board of a local Y camp where they had an annual women's wellness weekend. I served on that board for three years, eventually coordinating the event. I met many wonderful people through this volunteer activity. Volunteering is an important spiritual practice for grief because it shifts attention away from personal suffering and toward the needs of others.

I went online and joined every relevant meet-up group I could find: movie groups, social groups, walking groups, and more. One of the most stimulating groups was the Annapolis Connections Over Coffee, consisting of women who had professional interests similar to my own. I was thrilled to discover that the founder of the Connections Over Coffee series and Woman of the Year for the state of Maryland was a native West Virginian! Eventually, there were too many groups to fit in my schedule and I had to eliminate most of them. But initially, those groups helped me structure my time and develop networks of friends and other area professionals.

Although I'd met a lot of people, I hadn't made any real friends. At Nordstrom one day, while trying to figure out the best product for under-eye puffiness, I initiated a conversation with the sales clerk. I discovered she lived in my neighborhood. As women do, we networked. When she learned I was a therapist, she said, "Oh, you have to meet my next-door neighbor. She works at the University of Maryland and is some kind of a therapist too."

I felt so desperate to meet someone with similar interests that I marched over one block to this person's house, knocked on her door, and brashly introduced myself. She welcomed me graciously into her home with the most magnanimous smile.

"Oh hi, I'm glad to meet you. I'm Marie."

As it turned out, she'd moved to our neighborhood several years earlier from the DC area and hadn't made friends here either. She was just as pleased to meet me and we've become good friends.

Another day, while walking on our beach, I met another neighbor, Tessa. She was kind and gracious and included me in many of her neighborhood social events. Eventually, I learned she was a member of a long-standing book club she invited me to join. I met people in that club and also read a lot of books I wouldn't have read on my own, which stretched me.

Sea-Glass Collecting and Renewal

In my second year in Maryland, things continued to open up for me. I became utterly entranced with my abundant sea-glass collection. I'd found some beautiful pieces on our beach. I couldn't explain my attraction until I discovered it was a symbol of renewal. Like sea glass, I'd been tossed in life's choppy seas, but over time my sharp edges became smooth and polished as I learned to weather many shifting tides. I located a bead shop that offered classes in wrapping sea glass. I enrolled, met some other engaging women, refined my craft of making sea-glass jewelry, and donated pieces of it to local fundraisers to support my new community. I recognized there was something quieting and meditative about taking a piece of sea glass in my left hand with a piece of wire in my right and slowly wrapping and looping the wire around the glass, first making a bail, curling the first end, starting the wrap, curling the second end, and finishing the piece. Wearing a cherished pendant reminds me that resilience can develop in the most turbulent of waters. And even though sea glass can look soft and crack under pressure, typically it feels quite strong to the touch.

Online Dating

By the beginning of my third year in Maryland, I decided to go online to date. This was a momentous decision. After Jay passed, even the idea of being with some other man felt so completely wrong that I could never imagine myself in that position. But by this point Jay had been gone for six years and I felt ready to try going out with someone to experiment with how that felt. I was clear on my profile that I wasn't interested in marriage. Instead, I viewed this as an opportunity to make friends and to open up to possibilities.

Suddenly, I felt very much as if I was back in college. I took a renewed interest in my physical appearance, lost a few pounds, changed hairdressers, became more interested in makeup, and took advantage of my fashionista daughter's advice on attire.

"Mom," Lisanne said, "you look so pretty and young. You need to get some cool jeans and tops and boots." I complied, much as a dutiful daughter might comply with a parental admonition, recognizing the role reversal occurring in the process.

All of this must have worked, because my profile started getting some hits. Of course, many of the hits were unacceptable. An older man who had lost his wife and wanted a replacement. A much younger man, clearly a player, who just wanted to be friends with benefits. Another man who wanted a sailing and smoking companion, despite the statement on my profile about my wellness orientation. And yet another man who posted his profile with pictures of his dog, clearly the apple of his eye. How could I compete with that?

Finally, I did agree to meet a man for lunch. This man, Andrew, was a widower. I thought we might have a few things in common. The day of the first date I dressed carefully and youthfully, cognizant of my daughter's advice. I felt quite strange driving to the Macaroni Grill to meet someone for a date. I was excited and yet apprehensive at the same time. Would I recognize him from his profile picture? Would he recognize me? I walked into the restaurant and found him waiting for me near the door. "Oh, hi," I exclaimed in a voice I didn't recognize as my own. "Are you Andrew?"

"Yes," he replied, and, "you must be Sherry."

As we followed the hostess to our table, I couldn't help but feel like running away. I kept being flooded with images of all the times Jay and I had eaten at restaurants, and the incompatibility of the images of eating with my beloved and now with some stranger I had only met online was almost too much to bear.

As we were seated, I soon recognized that my level of discomfort was quite minimal compared to his. I pride myself on being a good conversationalist and I really had to rely on those skills with Andrew, who seemed a tad depressed to me. He was very quiet during the meal, often looking down often at his plate, didn't initiate much conversation, and tended to answer my queries with monosyllabic responses. At the end of the meal, he walked me to my car and took me by surprise when he pulled me close to him in a huge bear hug. My body felt the drought from that kind of hug. *Wow*, I thought to myself, *he may not be a talker, but he sure knows how to hug.*

Andrew had lost his wife of forty-five years a year after Jay died, and I surmised both of us were a bit lonely and starved for some physical contact with the opposite sex. The hug was sufficient for me to accept his dinner invitation for a second date. We continued to date for a year but, largely due to differences in values and worldviews, went our separate ways.

Subsequently, I entered into a more serious relationship with another man I met online, Fred. He and I had many things in common. But, over time, it became clear our paths were taking different turns and geographical locations, so Fred and I also parted ways.

While both divorced and widowed persons have experienced a relationship loss, I suspect the dating and reentry into subsequent relationships is a different process. Prior to being married to Jay, I had also been married and divorced. Divorced persons usually are looking for someone different from their ex. Widowed persons who have been happily married may be looking for someone similar to their late spouse. Divorcees are searching for a relationship that's much more positive than their marriage and often feel a sense of failure. Widowed persons may carry the image of their happy marriage into the dating scene, as well as their fear that they'll lose another spouse as well, should they remarry.

Seeking a Writing Project

In many ways, my life felt complete, but I was missing one piece. I felt called to write a book about healing from loss. I'd kept a journal since Jay's passing to jot down events, dreams, and insights. Often, I'd recommended expressive writing to some of my clients. Writing about stressful events has both physical and emotional benefits.[8]

I'd learned of a local author, Laura Oliver, who taught a class in writing life stories at St. John's College in Annapolis. I'd read her book, *The Story Within*, and I knew she could help me bring my story to life.[9] I intended to sign up for a semester class with her sometime during the year.

One early Monday morning, I was sitting in my new dental office as an emergency. I noticed another woman sitting there, writing vigorously in a notebook. I could tell she was in a lot of discomfort as she kept shifting around in her seat and covering her mouth with her hand. Still talking to everyone I met here, and hoping to distract her from her obvious discomfort, I began a conversation.

"Oh, are you by any chance a teacher?"

"No, I'm in a writing group and working on a piece for the group. In fact, the group is meeting at my house today, but I broke my front teeth this weekend and I'll miss our meeting," she lamented.

"I'm so sorry to hear about your teeth. You're really fortunate to be in a writing group. I'd like to find one here as I'm a newbie to Annapolis. I learned of someone named Laura Oliver who teaches at St. John's College and I thought I'd take her writing class this year."

"Well, Laura happens to be the writing coach for our group."

Eventually I became a member of that writing group, which has become the safe and cherished container for this story to emerge.

We Heal But Don't "Get Over" Grief

I don't ache for Jay now in the way I used to. I wake up content. Does that mean I or other grief survivors don't miss our beloved anymore? Or yearn for the way things were before our loss? Of course not. In the words of Anne Lamott, their absence is like a lifetime of homesickness we feel for them.[10] Holidays, anniversaries, and birthdays are still times of remembrance and longing. We heal from grief, but we don't *get over it*, as some who've never experienced deep loss might lead us to believe. Whenever we endure a significant loss, we carry the grief of it for the remainder of our days, even though our relationship to the loss itself will change. Someone I'm close to carries the pain of losing several stillbirth babies through miscarriage. Every time there's another miscarriage, it brings up the pain of the one before. And every time there's an anniversary of one of those miscarriages, she remembers not only the loss of the baby but also the loss of the dream of bearing a child. What we wanted but didn't have can be just as substantial a loss as losing someone or something precious.

No matter how much time has passed, memories of what used to be or reveries about what could have been remain. And grief is sneaky. Out of the blue, a song, a scent, a movie, a picture, can elicit grief over and over again. Earlier today, while sitting in a market, alone, eating lunch, I received a text from a friend about our neighbor, who had died suddenly. I'm not quite sure why—perhaps it was getting the news via text—but I fell apart. I started to cry and felt unbearably sad. My mind immediately turned to the husband, adult children, and dog she left behind. The sadness persisted for several days, in part because loss has become an inevitable part of my worldview. In carrying our grief, it becomes the backdrop or context by which we view and review information. Someone else who received the same text message, without the context of grief, may not have been impacted by this news in the same way.

Grief Is Cyclical, Not Linear

For many years, we assumed that to heal from grief, we must pass through the stages enumerated by Elisabeth Kübler-Ross, such as denial, anger, and depression, in order to accept the loss we incurred.[11] Now we recognize that this so-called stage theory of grief isn't applicable to everyone dying or healing from grief. I believe healing from grief is cyclical rather than linear. Grief ebbs and flows, much like the tide of an ocean that comes in and goes out. At times, the waves of grief are small and contained, but on other occasions they are large and often overwhelming but not necessarily crippling. Healing from grief isn't about exorcising it, but integrating it. Grief is integrated when we can open our hearts again to the world around us. This requires making ourselves vulnerable once again, acknowledging that love involves penetrability and heartbreak is a part of life.

Honoring Grief without Indulging in It

We must honor our grief without indulging in it. We must recognize our distress but not allow it to consume us. Instead, it must cycle through like the waves, coming in to our lives but going back out to sea.

I know of someone whose husband left her some years ago. Few folks want to be around her because she's turned into a chronic complainer about all kinds of things. The bitterness of her loss has extended into all areas of her life. She has become *small* as a result of the hand life dealt her, increasing her suffering and decreasing her choices. Her loss informs everything about her life and she has become victimized by it. This woman, like others, lost her spouse; others have lost a parent or child, a job or house. In war-torn areas, some folks even lose their town or country. Some people lose a sense like vision or hearing or some other ability or health status. Other people grow up with so little that loss is pervasive across all domains of their lives. As my yoga teacher here says, we all have our *junk*. Loss doesn't make us special. We don't distinguish ourselves by what or who we've lost; we only distinguish ourselves by how we heal from loss and whether we allow grief to destroy us or teach us.

To heal from grief, we have to restory our lives, to draw from narrative therapy. We have to imagine new beginnings and recreate new endings.

Of course, I was discovering some hurdles in that process.

8

LETTING GO AND FACING LOSS: STRESS AND SELF-CARE

Equanimity is always present, even in the midst of the most tumultuous and challenging circumstances.[1]
—Richard Miller

During Jay's illness and after his death, I recognized I was experiencing a stressful trauma. The fact that my dad died three months prior to
my husband added to my overall sense of vulnerability. As Jim Rendon
suggested in his book *Upside*, loss and grief are experienced as traumatic stress by many people.[2]

While there are many effects of chronic stress, one has to do with
the experience of cellular deterioration and telomeres. Telomeres are
protective casings at the end of a DNA strand. Elizabeth Blackburn and
Elissa Epel compare telomeres to the plastic caps on shoelaces.[3] When
the caps wear down, the shoelaces can't do their job effectively. Over
time, telomeres shorten and cells age and die, a process known as senescence. Shorter telomeres have been linked to a number of emotional and physical health problems. Research by Blackburn and Epel has
shown that chronic stress can shorten telomeres.[4] Some of this research
has been conducted with caregivers. While a longer length of caregiving
is related to shorter telomeres, perception of stress also impacts telomeres. Caregivers who didn't consider themselves that stressed weren't
impacted in the same way as those who reported severe stress.

How do we take care of ourselves while giving excellent support to our loved one? What dimensions of self-care are important as we face loss? And why? Psychologists and immunologists have discovered that lifestyle factors can promote cellular longevity. A strong social network, exercise, mindfulness training, and emotional regulation are some of the primary evidence-based interventions for increasing telomere length.[5] In their book *The Telomere Effect*, Blackburn and Epel offer a number of suggestions for ways to counteract chronic stress and improve telomeres.[6] In the following sections of this chapter, I'll make recommendations for ways you can resupply your empty tank, drained by the chronic stress of caregiving and bereavement.

Taking Care of Your Body

Loss engenders stress and stress wreaks havoc on the body by raising cortisol levels. Over time, this can result in a number of physical symptoms. Because I had experienced a chronic illness earlier in my life, I'd learned how to take care of my body. I knew the importance of eating vegetables and stepped this up. Kale and broccoli became daily staples, as did quinoa. (My cholesterol levels, while never high, enjoyed a nice drop!) I researched food choices for Jay, who began drinking concoctions of fresh vegetable juices mixed with protein powder. I discovered that small amounts of protein eaten judiciously throughout the day are linked to lower anxiety levels. Because my anxiety was at an all-time high, I ate protein at each meal and snacked on protein items such as nuts and almond butter. Both Jay and I reduced our dependence on caffeinated products and increased our intake of water to detoxify and hydrate our bodies. I worked diligently with him to reduce his cravings for sugar because some evidence suggests that sugar depresses the immune system and feeds cancer cells. I don't know how successful I was. When Jay realized death was imminent, he made a last-minute confession. "Honey," he exclaimed, still able to talk at that point, and in his deeply resonant voice, "when you clean out my man cave, I hid some doughnuts in the tool cabinet!"

I also recognized the value of exercise. I knew the research; regular exercise impacts the neurotransmitters in the brain that regulate mood and sleep and also increases telomere length. Exercise is an evidence-based intervention for reducing stress, anxiety, and depression. But there were days when working out was the last thing I wanted to do. On those days, though, I knew it was even more important to exercise and would will myself to get to the gym. The banner in my gym motivated me: "If you don't take care of your body, where will you live?" When I got in a funk, I always felt better after I worked out or rode my bike, walked, or danced. Moving the body releases stuck and stagnant energy. I'm not alone in this assessment; a recent study of over ten thousand participants found that people who are more physically active are happier. Moreover, they're happier in the very moments in which they're more physically active, whether they're completing an exercise program, standing, walking, or moving in some other fashion.[7]

I also supplemented my workouts with the community of yoga. I'd been a student of yoga for some time. During this tense time, I often went to two classes a week, one of which was a restorative yoga class designed especially for folks like me who found themselves mired in a mud bath of stress. Like exercise, yoga enjoys a mountain of empirical data supporting its effectiveness for a variety of physical and emotional conditions, of which stress is a huge one. Iyengar, the founder of one school of yoga, said, *"Yoga teaches us to cure what need not be endured and endure what cannot be cured."* His quote registered profoundly with the very external circumstance in which I found myself with Jay's cancer diagnosis and eventual death.

Increasing Connections with Others

Our physical and emotional well-being is also impacted by our social/interpersonal world. There's no doubt that chronic loneliness can be a killer. Loneliness is linked to higher stress hormones and earlier mortality.[8] If, during loss, you're feeling very alone, see it as a huge wake-up call and take action. Being socially isolated during a time of trauma or high stress makes the experience far worse. Do whatever it takes to break out of your social isolation. If you're lonely and over fifty, you may find help in the new AARP Connect2Affect site at *connect2affect.org*. If you are under fifty and lonely, check out Oprah Winfrey's *Just Say Hello* campaign, which allows us to connect via social media and/or Skype. Recognize that reaching out to others is probably easier for women than men, who may keep their grief to themselves, cut off old friends, or even commit to a rebound situation too soon after a loss just to mitigate loneliness.

After Jay died, I made a list of people I knew I could call, either because I needed social and emotional support or because I needed information or advice. I kept that list posted on the fridge, and every time I felt alone I looked at it. Just looking at the list helped me realize there were people in my corner who loved and supported me and would bend over backward to help in any way they could. I was fortunate to have a large network of friends because I'd lived in a small college town most of my adult life. Several of my friends had also experienced heart-wrenching losses and were especially helpful to me during this time. According to Rendon, in *Upside*, bonding with those who get what you're going through seems to be particularly healing after a traumatic loss. [9]

Loss and Relationships with Children

Shortly before Jay died, my youngest daughter, Lisanne, had secured her first real postcollege position, which required a move to Rhode Island for eight weeks of training, followed by a move to Albany, New York, for the actual job. We had a conversation a few days before she was to leave. "Mom," she asked, "what do you really think? Should I go to Rhode Island and try to do this, or should I just stay here with you for a while?" My heart wanted to say, *Stay*, but the therapist and mom in me actually said, "I'll be fine. You need to go." If I could have a redo of this situation, I would have scratched the inner therapist and mom and gone with my heart and said, *Stay*. Ultimately, I think her departure postponed some of the grieving process for both of us because the geographical distance prevented us from using our emotional bonds to help each other heal.

When a family member dies, the survivors face a changed existence and children need as much support as adults. Family survivors of all ages experience loss of security and familiarity when a family member passes away. Children need the surviving parent to provide "care, continuity, and connection." [10] Children grieve in different ways than adults.

Some widowed adults may expect their children to become substitutes for the lost companionship. Yet as Karen Rook and Susan Charles observe, this substitution often proves to be a mixed blessing, full of ambivalence and obligation.[11] I had an older friend who moved into the house of her adult daughter following the loss of her husband and, over time, lamented the lack of relationships among persons her own age. Her daughter resented the constant expectations from her mother for social connection. Relying on our children for companionship can over-burden them during their bereavement.

And navigating relationships with adult children is tricky in the best of times, but during traumatic loss when everyone's emotions are "messy," it's fraught with challenges! Most of us feel quite conflicted about these emerging relationships. We don't want to be a burden, yet we need their support and often they need ours. I found many useful tips for cultivating positive relationships with our daughters in a book written by Dr. Ruth Nemzoff, *Don't Bite Your Tongue: How to Foster Rewarding Relationships with Your Adult Children.*[12] As she astutely points out, the older we become, the more help we may need from our adult children. When adult children turn away, this can as be as damaging to a parent as when they reject our assistance or support.

Finding Contact with a Pet/Animal Companion

Several months after Jay died, Lisanne was visiting from her new job in Albany for Memorial Day weekend. We stumbled on a four-year-old golden retriever girl whose owners were trying to place her in a new home due to an impending move. Lisanne and I adopted her immediately and enjoyed seeing her fetch tennis balls and make immediate friends with our neighbors.

Abbey (whose name means *safe haven*) had been through her own kind of traumatic loss. When she was younger, she grew up in a house with Winston, a chocolate lab. The family divorced and Winston and Abbey were split up, with Winston being adopted by one family and Abbey by the family who gave her to us. Despite whatever trauma she had been through, she was a faithful, appreciative, and loving friend until she developed a brain tumor and passed away too young for her youthful spirit. Many days, Abbey and I had conversations about our losses. She would lay her sixty-pound body on her padded soft brown luxury bed and I would lay my head on her torso, often crying, "Abbey, do you miss Winston?" Her big brown, saucer-like eyes seemed to turn mournful. "I miss Jay so much," I'd confess to her. "Will I ever feel better?" I took solace in the fact that despite Abbey's loss of Winston, she now seemed like the happiest dog in the world. Whenever we'd walk together in a public place and greet people, they often said, "Your dog's smiling at me!" And she was!

Pets can be a wonderful addition for personal networks, especially for those who have more limited social support. People who are already part of groups or organizations such as a work, church, or school setting often have greater interpersonal resources to rely on after loss. But, especially for those who aren't joiners, or who live alone, rescuing a pet is good medicine for both the animal and the person.

Learning Something New

It may seem unusual to think about taking care of yourself intellectually during times of stress, trauma, and loss, yet this was a domain that was very important to both Jay and me as we progressed through his diagnosis and illness. Information-seeking became prevalent. When Jay couldn't sleep from chemo effects, he was often up in the night doing various Google searches about things that interested him. I, on the other hand, was doing Google searches about esophageal cancer, the immune system, and various effects of treatments. Both Jay and I continued to work during this period and I think work sustained us because it was a helpful distraction. I've often second-guessed our decision to do this. If we had known he would die in six months, would it have been better for us to have pulled back, stopped working, and lived somewhere on a beach? I don't think so. I think the fact that we had our routines was comforting, and we were both stimulated intellectually by our work.

I also joined Facebook and discovered social media to be a significant way to connect with people and even to learn things. I came to realize that intellectual self-care plays a large role in the healing of grief because of the role of learning and curiosity. New learning and sadness are incompatible. Perhaps that's because the impetus for learning something new and different is curiosity. Todd Kashdan, in his book *Curious?*, recommended being a "curious explorer" as an antidote to anxiety and as a precursor to developing a fulfilling life with purpose.[13] During some of my most anxious moments, I was able to turn down the anxiety by turning up my curiosity: *What's my role in life now? What happens after you die?* *What makes me feel most alive now?* Just as learning and sadness are incompatible, so are anxiety and curiosity. So, turn up your curiosity knob, use Google and social media liberally, start listening to TED talks and podcasts while you cook dinner or commute to work, and spend time discovering and learning about what fascinates you. You may find this will lead you to new adventures you never anticipated before your loss.

Developing Spiritual Practices

Finally, addressing your spiritual needs during stress and loss is so vital that it's hard to imagine how someone manages loss without exploring spiritual practices. Spirituality is defined in various ways. Some people are sustained by religious practices such as prayer and particular religious beliefs. People who have religious or spiritual practices are often better able to find meaning in a loss event. Jay was an ordained United Methodist minister in addition to being a licensed professional counselor and sought the counsel of two of his divinity school colleagues. I know contact with these colleagues was extremely important to him in reviewing his life and in preparing him emotionally to die with grace and peace.

I found spiritual sustenance in the practice of mindfulness and meditation. Contemplative prayer is often considered a form of meditation. I'd been a meditator prior to Jay's diagnosis to help manage my workload stress. After his diagnosis, I meditated even more frequently. There's voluminous data suggesting that regular meditation retrains the brain, helping us become more optimistic and less impacted by stressful circumstances.[14] Grief and trauma can cause the brain and the autonomic nervous system to become dysregulated, and meditation is a primary way to move from a state of threat to a place of healing. Typically, I meditated in a more traditional way, focusing on my breath and a calming mantra such as "Breathe in peace" and "Breathe out stress." Sometimes I meditated with a calming counting breath, inhaling to the count of four, exhaling to the count of six or even eight. This is an important practice for self-calming because a longer exhalation stimulates the vagus nerve and elicits the parasympathetic nervous system, which slows down the heart rate and blood pressure and promotes relaxation.

While contemplative prayer and meditation worked well for me, other people may find comfort in different spiritual practices that are consistent with their cultural and religious beliefs. A deeply religious African American friend of mine who recently lost his wife to cancer confided that listening to a sermon every day on his Sirius radio while driving gave him the necessary mindset to continue to work and care for his sons despite his bereavement.

My meditation practice shifted a few years after Jay died when I participated in a training workshop conducted by Richard Miller, a psychologist and yoga teacher who founded a center called the Integrative Restorative Institute. This weekend training on the beautiful grounds of Duke University, where Jay had attended divinity school, introduced me to the practice of iRest (short for Integrative Restoration). This evidence-based practice, which has been used and researched for over twenty-five years, involves deep relaxation and guided meditative inquiry. [15] It's been endorsed by the surgeon general's office as a complementary and alternative medicine (CAM) approach to well-being. It's a practice that's integrative in that it heals unresolved wounds, traumas, and issues in the body and mind, and restorative as it calms the mind amid the ever-changing circumstances of life.

In his soft, soothing voice in a windowed, light-filled room with nature-inspired themes at the Duke Integrative Medicine Center, Richard described the benefits of this research-based practice that has been used extensively with veterans with PTSD and in hospices and cancer outpatient clinics. As we lay on our backs on mats on the floor, he led us through several varying practices during the weekend, and tears welled up in my eyes as I heard him say, *Remember you have the capacity to meet, greet, and restore from any circumstance in your life.* This phrase in particular helped me believe I could and would heal from sadness and hopelessness. There's scarcely a day now that goes by that I don't meditate to the sound of his calming voice on his *Resting in Stillness* CD.[16] With continued practice, I have witnessed marked changes in my ability to self-soothe and maintain equanimity in the face of crises, making the Maryland University of Integrative Health mantra, *"Upset is optional,"* a feasible goal and intention. I love their mantra, particularly in light of new findings that venting of upsets can be deleterious to our health. Moreover, as Linda Graham points out, each time we become "reactive," we reinforce a particular pattern of neural firing in our brains, increasing our suffering.[17] Maintaining equanimity as fostered by iRest strengthens new and different neural patterns that are calming.

My sadness often shifted to anger and, as a Christian, I felt angry with God. I remember saying to a ministerial colleague of Jay's, "How could God have let this happen to him?" I was *pissed off* that he was taken away from me too soon. I was mad that I was sad and I was mad that our daughters were upset and had been deprived of precious years with their wonderful father and stepfather. In his book *Upside*, Rendon explains this is a common reaction to traumatic loss because we've developed a core sense of ourselves or an assumptive self based on a worldview in which we feel safe and protected.[18] Loss and trauma tear down this assumptive self when bad things happen to us. *Why me?* or *What did I do to deserve this?* are common questions with no real answers that reflect ways in which the loss has disrupted our sense of the world and our safety in it. Collectively, as a country, almost everyone in the United States experienced this in varying degrees on 9/11, an event that shattered our worldviews and assumptions about safety and predictability in a unique and disturbing way.

Thankfully, these feelings of anger and loss of safety eroded over time and were gradually replaced with what can only be described as gratitude. I'm grateful that Jay was in my life and grateful for all the ways in which his being on earth enriched my life and the lives of so many others his presence graced. There's a pottery jar labeled "Blessings" that Jay and I received as a gift. This blue-green jar sits on my black pearl kitchen counter with Post-it notes and a pen at its side. Often, I jot down an awareness of something or someone I feel grateful for and place the Post-it note in the jar. *My daughter called me today on her break and it was wonderful to hear her voice. My vet taking care of Abbey is so kind. Went on a new hike today with my neighbor, so glad I'm mobile enough to do it.* If I start to feel like a victim instead of a survivor, I take the notes out of the jar, reread them, and meditate on the many ways in which my life continues to be privileged and graced despite the losses. This is one of the ways I've learned to cope with anger and use my feelings as a positive rather than a negative force in my life.

TAKING CHARGE OF YOUR FEELINGS AND THOUGHTS

The condition of the body impacts our emotional health just as our emotional health impacts our physiology. Deeply felt emotions are often stored in the body and can resurface at a later time in the form of illness.[19] And no doubt about it, my emotions were registering on my body. Not only was my sleep disrupted, but I developed canker sores all over my mouth, and I found it challenging to resist crying at the first little daily stressor that appeared during Jay's illness. From the moment I received the news about Jay's diagnosis, I lived with a pit in the bottom of my stomach. Regulation of emotions, or *affect regulation*, is a huge part of what brings clients to psychotherapy. I had worked for years with clients on helping them regulate their feelings; now my own were spinning out of control.

In my clinical practice, I worked a lot with clients dealing with affect-regulation issues from a cognitive perspective; that is, how you think and what you think strongly impacts how you feel. As the Greek philosopher Epictetus said, *"It's not what happens to you but how you react to it that matters."* But as hard as I tried to apply cognitive therapy to my own distressing thoughts, I couldn't do it. Well, I tried doing it, but initially I didn't see much effect. My feelings of bereftness were too strong.

I got some relief from reading a book by Pema Chodron, *When Things Fall Apart: Heart Advice for Difficult Times.*[20] Her book introduced me to the teachings of Buddhism and the concepts of impermanence and suffering. I recognized that, in her words, Jay and I "had a beautiful plan and it didn't work out." As a result, I was panic-stricken and lost. I started meditating to let this story line go. When that got tough, I would chant Lao Tzu's mantra to myself: *"If you realize things all change, there is nothing you will try to hold on to."*

LETTING GO OF OLD STORY LINES

With perspective, I realized the role that my expectations played in creating and maintaining my emotional distress. As Anne Lamott said in a Facebook post, "Expectations are resentments under construction."[21] When I married Jay, I expected him to be healthy. I expected him to live a long life. After all, he had rarely visited a doctor. I, on the other hand, was plagued for most of our married life with chronic sinus and bronchial infections, headaches, and fatigue. I expected the two of us to grow old together and enjoy a later life of leisure, travel, and less financial stress. I expected his strength to bolster mine as we aged together and lived the happily-ever-after myth. All these expectations were blown away with his cancer diagnosis. In the decade since Jay's passing, I've worked hard to recognize and let go of illusions and attachments to expectations.

The Dalai Lama has said that holding on to things and people we believe will endure forever creates most of our suffering around loss. I resisted letting go of Jay. I hated how I could feel his body shut down a little more each day during his last month of life while he was in the inpatient hospice unit. During my daily multiple visits there, I climbed into bed with him, holding on to him for dear life—*my* life, I might add. After he died, I hated coming home from work to an empty house, silent except for the echo of my footsteps. I hated having to figure out the intricacies of the garage door opener, which only seemed to function when Jay was operating it. I hated going out into the freezing, windy cold weather to shovel snow off the driveway when I was accustomed to staying inside and fixing hot spiced tea or hot chocolate to greet Jay after he finished that onerous task.

But what's more accurate is that the deeper lesson for me was letting go of my resistance to the situation itself, a situation I hadn't created, nor was it one I could control or fix. I was mad Jay got cancer. After all, he had reassured me every time I got on his case about his sugar fixes or his work stress or his lack of sleep that he would *never* get cancer because, he said, "It doesn't run in my family." I was angry with myself that I bought into this illusion, and I was angry with his cavalier attitude about his invincibility. I was upset that his cancer was fast-growing, aggressive, and in an inoperable place in his body. On the day he was diagnosed, I had trouble letting go of my hair appointment, scheduled for the next day, because in an instant, my tightly planned life was rapidly unraveling and I had no clue what was coming next. *How dare cancer disrupt our life like this?* was the predominant thought in my ego-centered head.

Facing Loss: Resisting or Yielding

According to Eckhart Tolle, when loss occurs, we have two basic choices: we can resist or we can yield.[22] If we resist, any action we take creates even more resistance. That's because resistance sharpens our focus on what we *don't* want. If we yield, the act of surrender and of letting go promotes acceptance and a newer awakening in ourselves, a different consciousness about who we are and the situation in which we find ourselves.

How does the letting go following loss inform our lives as we struggle to make sense of it and also move ahead in a different, more conscious way? When we really understand the concept of impermanence, we recognize that trying to hold on to something or someone already lost is both an illusion and an exercise in futility.

Laozi, the ancient Chinese mystic and author of *Tao Te Ching*, observed: "*Watch your thoughts; they become words. Watch your words; they become actions. Watch your actions; they become habits. Watch your habits; they become character. Watch your character; it becomes your destiny.*" We fuel our distress by telling ourselves the same sad stories over and over instead of letting them go. I choose my thoughts, and the thoughts I select can make me feel better or worse about a tough situation or a hard place to live.

Restorying: Finding a Healthy Narrative

Donald Meichenbaum asserts that it's precisely the *nature* of the kind of thoughts and stories we create that either fuels distress or resilience after a catastrophic loss or event.[23] His therapeutic modus operandi to helping loss survivors "restory" is called *Constructive Narrative Perspective* or CNP. It's an approach designed to help people develop healing stories with accompanying useful coping skills. When we suffer a loss or endure a catastrophe, and create a story line in which we are the victim with no control over the outcome, we are likely to become hypervigilant about danger and threats, engage in countless hours of unproductive ruminations, and have difficulty making decisions or resolving issues because of our resulting helplessness and hopelessness.[24] In contrast, when we can rewrite our story and incorporate a measure of redemption such as a positive emotion, a sense of gratitude, a forgiving attitude, humor, an identification of something we did to cope, altruism, and/or mindfulness, we let go of what cannot be changed, we accept what has changed, and transform our disempowerment into empowerment.[25]

Narratives of Involuntary and Voluntary Losses

Sometimes our story lines are different and mostly positive or mostly negative, depending on whether the loss we mourn is involuntary or voluntary. Some losses that happen to us are involuntary, not chosen. Losing a family member to death or dementia, having a job taken away, losing an election, losing healthy bodily functions with aging, having a beloved walk out after a long-standing relationship—these are losses that happen to us that are usually out of our control. Other kinds of losses are voluntary, even intentional. We can choose to leave a position or a relationship or a community that no longer fulfills us.

The challenges in letting go of involuntary and voluntary losses may be different. Involuntary losses can be harder to accept because something has happened to us. We're in shock and disbelief. Our ego-centered minds struggle. *How can this be happening to me now? What did I do to deserve this loss?* Rabbi Kushner's words, "How can bad things happen to good people?" often apply in this situation.[26] Whenever something or someone precious is taken away from us, though, we still have choices about the ultimate outcome or ending of the story. We can attach to self-pity, anger, and bitterness, or we can let go of these cantankerous feelings and open ourselves to the opportunities and growth that arise because of the loss. That's easier said than done, of course. Every painful loss we have serves us in some way if we can stay open and patient enough to bear witness to its effects. Mark Nepo reminds us of this: "For only when we can outwait the dark will the sharpness of experience recede like a tide to reveal what has survived beneath it all."[27]

Voluntary losses often go down easier, are less difficult to swallow, but present their own challenges in letting go, primarily because of our attachments. The stronger the attachment, the greater our loss. A family I know struggled to let go of their wife and mother when leukemia came back in her bones following a bone marrow transplant. Despite the fact that she was in uncontrolled pain and agony, they still wanted to continue more treatment, prolonging *her* suffering. Choosing to leave a place of employment, a relationship, a friendship, a community or neighborhood, or letting go of someone on life support may feel like the right thing to do, yet saying good-bye to someone or something we have attached to is never an easy thing.

Letting Go and Self-Differentiation

I've accomplished letting go to some degree by trying to live in a much more *self-differentiated* fashion than I did prior to losing Jay. "Self-differentiation" is a term borrowed from cellular biology by the renowned family therapist Murray Bowen.[28] As it pertains to relationships, self-differentiation is the ability to experience closeness with and also independence from another person. On a continuum from greater to lesser self-differentiation, highly differentiated people are psychologically healthier, report more satisfying intimate partnerships, and are more effective problem solvers. Less differentiated people have more chronic anxiety and are more dysfunctional under stress, often becoming either overly compliant and codependent or dogmatic and counterdependent. Being well differentiated indicates that I have a realistic sense of dependence on others but can remain calm in the face of conflict, criticism, and rejection so I can think clearly and avoid emotional reactivity. It suggests I'm less at the mercy of the feelings of the moment. It means I can remain emotionally connected to others and not cut them off, while realizing I'm my own person, with thoughts and feelings unique to me and different from others. It also implies I recognize the only person I can control or fix is me.

The authors of *The Self Under Siege* describe several possible ways to achieve greater self-differentiation.[29] These steps include identifying negative inner voices about oneself, others, and the world that aren't our thoughts but rather things we internalized from our early caretakers. The task is to tame our inner critic so it no longer controls our actions. Another step these authors recommend is to develop our own voice that reflects a distinct moral compass and set of values we subscribe to, not just what we adopted from our family of origin.

I feel differentiated enough now to know that I will survive a voluntary loss and certainly learn from it. How? I don't fuse or overidentify with thoughts, feelings, plans, and people in such a way that when they go, I lose myself in the process. Of course, I may feel sad, but I'm still intact. One of the ways that the losses of Jay and my parents served me was to help me identify and let go of situations and people I was involved with who were not good for me. It's almost as if these hard, sudden, involuntary losses fortified me like a megavitamin dose, making the phrase "Respect yourself enough to walk away from situations that no longer serve you, grow you, or make you peaceful" especially relevant. Now, when I choose to let go of things or people that no longer serve me, I'm not as devastated as I would have been before.

Do these lessons and experiences mean we should never attach to anybody or anything so that ultimately there's nothing to ever let go of? No. Healthy attachment is part of hope, ambition, and even psychological health. But healthy attachment is different from the illusion that our life will not go on without the presence of this person, object, or situation in it. Healthy attachment is being connected without being clingy. Still, there will always be things for us to let go of, and loss is ever present, perhaps even necessary at times, as Judith Viorst so aptly reminded us in her wise book *Necessary Losses*.[30] There will always be connections we value and, ultimately, some of these connections will fade or be severed.

But the lessons I hope I've learned involve letting go of expectations and plans when they don't turn out the way I wanted, and letting go of resistance to accepting losses I don't like or didn't create. Attaching my well-being to these expectations, and suffering when such expectations aren't met, takes energy away from living fully in the present, the only moment I'm guaranteed to have. The truest lesson I've learned from loss is that life is short and comes with no extended warranties. So, I choose to live my life now as fully and as graciously as possible, celebrating each moment and each breath I take, as an affirmation that I'm still alive in this world and that my life counts for something.

9

COPING WITH LOSS: GRIEF SURVIVORS

The world breaks everyone and afterward many are stronger at the broken places. [1]
—Ernest Hemingway

Jim, a man in his late sixties whose wife died suddenly three months ago, contacted me recently. He said, "I still talk to Betty all the time, but when she doesn't answer, my pain is unbearable. What can I do to fix this?"

According to Pauline Boss and Donna Carnes, the Western idea that we get closure after loss and move on is a myth that ends up creating more suffering than it alleviates. [2] They note that particularly in US culture, we're so uncomfortable with loss and suffering that we just want to move beyond it. While we don't want to drown in grief, the ultimate goal is to learn to live with it, not remove it. A more realistic recovery from loss involves experiencing ups and downs over time. Trying to give grief and sorrow a time limit and a completion date is both "unreasonable" and "unfair." [3]

I recall attending an event for someone who was retiring from a long-held job. In the goodbye speech, this man teared up when mentioning the name of his youngest daughter, who was killed suddenly in an accident a number of years before. This didn't surprise me because sadness after loss often erupts at emotionally charged moments. Sadness is different from depression, which is conceptualized and treated as a cognitive, behavioral, and biochemical condition. Sadness is a human emotion and a natural expression of grief following the loss of something or someone valuable. Sadness is an expression of our human condition, and often the deeper the attachment, the more profound the sadness. We learn to live with loss by allowing our sadness to coexist with moments of joy. As the Vietnamese Buddhist monk Thich Nhat Hanh said, *"Without the mud, you cannot grow the lotus flower."*

Staying in the Gap

Elizabeth Lesser, in her insightful book *Broken Open*, recounts how stunned she was by the sheer size of space left after the sudden death of her father.[4] She wanted to fill the space immediately with work, friends, and travel, but her intuition suggested otherwise. She took time off from work and allowed herself to sit with the sadness. She wanted to experience something she'd learned from the Lutheran theologian Dietrich Bonhoeffer called *the gap*.[5] Bonhoeffer writes:

> Nothing can make up for the absence of someone whom we love, and it would be wrong to try to find a substitute; we must simply hold out and see it through. This sounds very hard at first, but at the same time, it is a great consolation, for the *gap*, as long as it remains unfilled, preserves the bonds between us.[6]

It was challenging for Lesser to live in the gap following her father's death. She had long conversations with her departed father that surprised her because they'd had a "complex" relationship. Still, she cultivated patience and waited while simultaneously storing up healing energy. Lesser describes how the veil of grief eventually lifted and she noticed a new kind of energy, some of which she attributed to her late father. These reservoirs of healing energy become important for the exploration of new opportunities.[7]

Lesser cites the following poem from Rumi as a metaphor for waking up after sitting in the gap:

> *Today, like every other day, we wake up empty*
> *And frightened. Don't open the door to the study*
> *And begin reading. Take down the dulcimer.*
> *Let the beauty of what you love be what you do.*
> *There are hundreds of ways to kiss the ground.*

Rumi speaks of despair and sadness but proposes a new way to bring healing energy to ourselves. Each of us can find some way of "taking down the dulcimer"; perhaps a walk in nature or a chat with a friend. In this chapter, I recommend ways to cope with loss and to recapture the sweetness of life comingled with sorrow, but only after you sit in the gap!

Create Intentions

Often people say, "I can't stand this aloneness I'm feeling after my divorce," or "I don't know what to do with myself now that I've retired or lost my job." We don't recognize that empty space is an important gift from loss. Much like sitting in the gap, we need times of quietude in our frenetic and overscheduled lives to create a new path. The unfilled space provides opportunities to make room for an idea to emerge, as all new beginnings start there.

As ideas materialize, we create intentions. For example, an intention of mine after Jay died was, *"I'm creating a life of significance even though I don't have a significant other."* An intention is a statement that reflects what we want, and we visualize it as an already accomplished fact. Our intentions create the pathway between our current situation and the future we want to create. Of course, particular circumstances of loss will dictate intentions. A friend of mine whose spouse was retiring noted that she experienced the loss of their coupleship as his intentions became *me* rather than *we* oriented. She wanted to develop intentions they could both embrace.

Our intentions gain momentum as we talk about them with others. When Jay was dying, and I was visualizing new directions for my life as a widow, I had conversations about my intentions with close friends and colleagues. Such conversations enable our future reality to become more concrete and are reassuring to our psyche. Many clients have come to see me precisely at this point in their grief journey as they need a safe place to feel heard. It's important to be selective about the people we talk with, choosing those who are supportive rather than judgmental or competitive.

Sometimes our intentions become cluttered with internal voices that undermine our fragile goals: *"Sherry, you'll be a mess. You'll never be able to function on your own without Jay. What makes you think you can do this?"* We need to root out these damaging messages, much like extinguishing a fire that, if allowed to smolder, can overtake a beautiful space. In *My Stroke of Insight,* Jill Bolte Taylor chronicles how such negative messages dropped out of her repertoire immediately following a stroke. Now, eight years later, when she notices negativity running through her mind, she stops it by saying to herself, *"I'm not interested in running that circuit."*[8]

Being with that uninhabited space helps us build and store precious energy we'll need to take a new step because, eventually, we have to move forward. This might mean circumventing negative people, sitting with unpleasant emotions until they pass, and letting go of negative internal voices and old beliefs. When we do this on a consistent basis, we create different mental pathways in the brain that reinforce our new thought patterns.

Plant Seeds of Resilience

A major way we plant seeds of resilience is to do things to enhance our well-being as loss challenges it. Well-being is a skill set that can be learned. Neuroscience reveals that to some extent, well-being is impacted by emotional styles. The work of neuroscientist Richard Davidson describes an emotional style as "a consistent way we respond to things that happen to us."[9] Emotional styles are governed by specific and identifiable circuits in our brains and impact our likelihood of experiencing particular feelings and moods and include such things as resilience, outlook, and self-awareness.[10] Brendon Burchard describes a number of ways he helped himself recover from a physical loss by creating a series of "triggers"; activities and reminders that helped him cultivate more positive energy and ways of being into his life, now changed by the brain injury he'd sustained.[11]

"Seeds" that are especially important to cultivate for resilience include meditation, nutrition, sleep, exercise, and social support.

Meditation

Resilience is a skill set and can be strengthened with practice. This is important because some recent research has found that resilience following the loss of a spouse may be less common than we'd surmised.[12] In her article "Bounce Back," Mandy Oaklander asserts there is no greater miracle for developing resilience than meditation.[13] In their book *Altered Traits*, Daniel Goleman and Richard Davidson review all the ways that regular practice of meditation changes your body and brain, including the rapidity from which seasoned meditators recover from stressful events.[14]

Meditation has been defined as "disciplined activities to augment awareness and to foster calming or stress relaxation responding."[15] There are many ways to meditate. Perhaps the simplest one is to engage in focused attention; sit quietly with your spine erect and follow your breath as you inhale and exhale. When your mind wanders, bring your attention back to your breath. If this proves too challenging, try an app to guide you such as *Calm.com, InsightTimer, HeadSpace, Breathe2Relax,* or *Tactical Breather.* Or Google your nearest location for training in an evidence-based approach for mindfulness developed by Jon Kabat-Zinn called *MBSR—Mindfulness Based Stress Reduction*—where you can learn how to do this in a group/class setting or on your device.[16] MBSR is a multicomponent practice that includes breath awareness, yoga, a body scan, and mindfulness of thoughts and feelings.[17] MBSR is efficacious for both stress and anxiety reduction.[18] If you attempt meditation on your own and experience feelings of agitation or dissociation, consider finding a skilled therapeutic practitioner who can assist you in this practice. And a caveat: if you practice mediation regularly, be sure to have your health-care provider monitor the dosage of any prescription medicines you take; your new state of calm may necessitate lower doses.

Exercise, Sleep, and Nutrition

While we understand that regular exercise, healthy foods, and sufficient sleep have a profound impact on our minds, Davidson points out that the lack of these sabotage our ability to regulate our thoughts, feelings, and behaviors.[19] *Shortchanging ourselves by eating or sleeping poorly and not moving our bodies means we are prone to mood instability and unhappiness.* I can attest to this. In the years since Jay has passed, my grief has often ebbed and flowed depending on the state of my body. On days when I haven't slept well or have overworked and forgotten to move around, deep sorrow erupts, making me feel doom and gloom. But on days when I've nourished and moved my body and slept like a baby, I can tackle almost anything.

Social Support

Another way to increase our well-being and resilience is to cultivate social support. I can't say it more clearly: of all potential possibilities, social support is the best predictor of health and happiness. Human connection leads to significant changes in brain functioning, while loneliness or social disconnection increases stress hormones and impairs executive functioning of the brain. *Sadness is helped most by ties to others.*[20] Our brains are hardwired to have at least one—and up to five—confidantes in our life, so part of healing our sorrow is to find others we can confide in. If the person you lost was your sole confidante in life, it's especially important to immediately find someone else you can talk to, even if that person might be a therapist, at least initially. If you want to join a grief support group and can't find one, try contacting a local hospice, funeral home, or hospital for suggestions. Reliable comfort or having someone to confide in following spousal loss is extremely important for developing resilience.[21]

Perhaps this is because grief itself is an experience of such profound disconnection. Rumi says, "There is a secret medicine given only to those who hurt so hard, they cannot hope. It is this: Look as long as you can at the friend that you love." Of course, we need to be selective in who we choose as friends and close companions. Happiness and unhappiness are contagious. Davidson concludes that we should pay close attention to the people we spend time around and even to the cultural messages we expose ourselves to; think social media and television.[22]

We can also develop habits to make our outlook more optimistic. While I've always been an optimistic person, my outlook took a plunge after Jay's terminal diagnosis and death. Eventually, I realized that working on my outlook didn't mean I had to become suddenly happy again, which felt unrealistic. Harvard psychologist Susan David says that forcing yourself to feel happy when you don't usually backfires.[23] Instead, my outlook improved when I was able to feel more *peaceful*.

Search for Meaning

One way we can achieve a better outlook in the face of tragedy is to search for meaning. While getting closure is usually impossible after a significant loss, finding meaning isn't. Boss and Carnes suggest that so much of the loss we experience is meaningless; we can't make sense of it or explain how a particular event happened to us. [24] Yet, as they note, we can tolerate something *meaningless* as long as we find something else that's *meaningful*. Meaning helps us learn to live with situations we feel powerless to manage or change.

As grief survivors, we do this in various ways. As noted above, relatedness and belonging improve our outlook and increase our sense that life is meaningful. [25] Having a spiritual practice or religious faith also increases our sense of meaning in life. If we've lost someone close to us, we usually create meaning by continuing to remember them with particular rituals to help us stay connected to our memories. We may celebrate their birthday or continue to set a place for them at the dining table. We may visit a grave on the anniversary date of the death and commemorate it with flowers, say a rosary for a year, or unveil a tombstone at the end of a year. We may collect their ashes in an urn or scatter them in beloved places. We may wear their picture in a locket close to our heart or create a shrine of pictures in our house. We may take remnants of their clothes and make a quilt we use to warm ourselves on cold, lonely winter evenings when our heart aches for their physical presence. We may create a scholarship in their memory. Rituals can help us establish a place in our lives to honor the connection of the person or even the place or relationship we've lost.

Contribution and Service

Often a way to find greater peace and meaning and ultimately improve our outlook is through contribution and service. Constructing a foundation, advocating for peace, or donating money to various causes such as cancer or dementia research are examples. Volunteering and mentoring are other powerful tools, especially in some way that helps our heart hurt less. I love dogs, especially golden retrievers, so my first volunteer experience after losing Jay was with an organization that trained these dogs as service animals. Later, I volunteered to coordinate a women's wellness retreat, an area of my clinical practice.

Another small but important way to contribute is to practice random acts of kindness. There's a "31 Days of Kindness" web-based challenge that includes such activities as writing a thank-you letter, picking up trash, buying someone a coffee, sending a letter to a soldier, letting someone go in line ahead of you, and so on. [26] Kira Newman believes that *stacking* acts of kindness by doing multiple actions on one day has a more profound effect than spreading this activity out across days.[27] She suggests performing five random acts of kindness one day per week during a six-week period and noticing what happens. If you feel stuck conjuring up potential acts of kindness, consult an app called Pay It Forward.

Contributing and volunteering have strong physiological and neurological benefits. Davidson has found that "doing good" is related to "feeling good."[28] This is important because one of the most robust predictors of meaning in life is positive affect or feeling good. When we feel good, we experience more meaning in life.[29] Grief and sadness can be self-absorbing. Volunteering, mentoring, and practicing kindness helped me take the focus off myself and turn it toward others.

The Practice of Gratitude

There may be no more significant way to change and improve our outlook than practicing gratitude on a daily basis. Gratitude is an experience of being thankful and is linked to better physical and emotional well-being, especially when we truly take the time to savor something good in our lives. Like contribution and service, gratitude helps us connect to others. Gratitude practice can be as simple as listing three things you feel grateful for that you've noticed during the day. Do this for a month and then see how your outlook has changed. One tip: this practice works best if you note *different* things each evening rather than writing the same three things as you retrain your brain to scan for positives instead of negatives. It's also important to be as specific as possible. Instead of *"I'm grateful for my friend Betty,"* I'll note *"I'm grateful for the kayak adventure that Betty encouraged me to take today."* Amy Gallo, writing about how to turn a bad day around, cites evidence suggesting it's hard to be depressed *and* grateful *simultaneously*.[30] She recommends turning your attention to something good as soon as you start to feel negative.

Shawn Achor, author of *The Happiness Advantage*, suggests a related activity he calls *The Doubler*.[31] For several minutes a day, recall one positive thing that's happened to you in the last twenty-four hours and bullet point or list each detail of the experience you can remember. Because the brain doesn't discriminate between real and imagined experience, Achor says we double our most meaningful experience in our brain by this experience. Achor cites research in which people with pain did this daily for six weeks and were able to cut their pain meds in half. Technology can help us practice gratitude. Just as Fitbits help ensure we take over ten thousand steps per day, the Pebblestone can be tapped to track each time we have a moment of gratitude.[32] *The Uplifter* is an app that features a gratitude journal.

Oprah Winfrey introduced the practice of gratitude journaling back in the late 1990s. Since then, there has been an explosion of research exploring the benefits of various kinds of gratitude practice. Neuroscience research indicates that the practice of daily gratitude stimulates the brain to produce more positive feelings and is connected to markers of well-being, perhaps because this practice shifts our brain's attention away from toxic emotions.[33] A study conducted by Prathik Kini et al. found that a simple gratitude-writing task produced changes in the brain that persisted over time and resulted in significantly better mental health in the participants over time.[34] Heart patients who kept gratitude journals for eight weeks had lower levels of inflammation.[35] Robert Emmons, a gratitude researcher, reports that gratitude practices improve sleep and physical activity, reduce excessive entitlement, and incentivize us to contribute more.[36]

I'll confess it was hard to feel grateful after losing Jay. Yet as Arthur C. Brooks noted in a *New York Times* article, it's when we *don't* feel grateful that it's most important to *be* grateful.[37] For me, the opposite of gratefulness is entitlement. I don't have easy remedies for this issue other than to suggest a prayer or mantra: *"God, or Goddess, this ucks. Help me see the bigger picture here and trust the process."* I don't think you can *will* your way into gratitude when it doesn't come easily. Naming your resistance to it and sitting with that resistance often provides an eventual opening for gratitude to appear. On hard days, I remembered that the monks and nuns from Tibet offer gratitude prayers even for their suffering! Remember, too, that the effects of gratitude practice on your mood and well-being may accrue over time.[38] Don't give up the practice just because you don't notice an immediate shift!

Connect with Nature

Sometimes when gratitude hasn't come easily for me, I've navigated my way into it by spending some time in nature. When living in West Virginia, walking in the hemlock forest or arboretum always helped me to experience gratefulness. In Maryland, kayaking on the creek or walking on the beach has the same effect. In Japan, people are advised to take walks in the woods among the trees for better health. This practice is appropriately called forest bathing (*shinrin-yoku*). Immersing yourself in nature is like a baptism, a practice that's profoundly spiritual in terms of restoration and renewal. Trees and plants emit aromatic compounds that can promote healthy physiological changes, much like aromatherapy can.[39]

In *The Healing Power of Nature*, Alexandra Sifferlin cites specific ways in which being in nature promotes well-being: lowering blood pressure, increasing cancer-fighting cells, assisting with attention deficit symptoms, and easing depression and anxiety.[40] Gregory Bratman et al. discovered that walking in nature quiets the brain and reduces ruminations and brooding.[41] This same effect isn't achieved by walking in an urban environment and is also cancelled by using technology. You can enhance the nature effects on your well-being by walking in a quiet environment without your technology, surrounded by lots of trees or water. Newman suggests taking a *savoring walk* to promote a positive outlook.[42] Walk for twenty minutes in nature and notice what you like. Take the time to be mindful to absorb and enjoy the experience around you. Even visualizing nature, or seeing pictures of trees out your window, putting a plant in your room, or listening to nature sounds, particularly birdsongs, increases well-being and reduces stress. Getting outside and getting sunshine are often very simple ways to improve our outlook that cost nothing. Florence Williams, in her book *The Nature Fix*, reports a "dose responsive" relationship between nature and well-being.[43] Although five hours a month in nature settings is considered the minimum for well-being, clearly the more time spent in nature, the better we feel.

Coping-with-Loss Guidelines

In addition to these general ideas, consider the following specific guidelines for coping with loss compiled from professional literature and my experiences. A caveat, though: everyone experiences grief and loss differently, so not all these ideas may work for you.

Reduce responsibilities.

Immediately after a loss, allow yourself to be like an infant. Give yourself the treat of at least an hour a day where you do nothing. Ask for as much as you need; accept help that's offered, and get as much support as you can find. *This is the time to do less, not more.*

Resist unwanted advice.

When life feels topsy-turvy, it's tempting to dwell on how to change it. With your change in status, other people will have much advice for you on topics ranging from a move to a job change to a new hobby or dating interest. Be discerning about taking advice from others, especially if it's unsolicited. Tune into yourself and listen to your gut.

Defer major decisions.

For most people, it's probably wise not to make any major decisions or commitments for at least a year after the loss, perhaps two. Often the second year following a loss is more tumultuous and harder to cope with than the first. We are often still in some form of shock in the early stages of loss, which challenges our decision-making skills.

Plan for grief triggers.

Remember that firsts of any kind are unusually challenging. The first holiday without your beloved, the first trip you take without your family member, and the first return to a place where the loss occurred are emotionally difficult. The first steps you take after a divorce or the loss of a job or home are difficult. A constant grief trigger for me has been in card shops, when it hits me that I no longer have a reason to buy a card anymore for a father, a mother, a husband, or a sister. Try to anticipate and plan for these days and find support. Prior preparation for these days and events is critical because avoiding grief triggers isn't helpful as it promotes avoidance behavior. Instead, find ways to engage in what triggers you, but do so in a way that makes it more pleasant. I still go to card stores and often look at funny cards instead as a way to cope with this potential trigger.

Identify vulnerabilities.

Grief can exacerbate things that make you feel vulnerable, afraid, or unsafe. I've always had a peculiar vulnerability about medical procedures, even when Jay was alive. Having to get an MRI on my knee once undid me so much that he accompanied me to the MRI site and waited until I was finished. When I had to undergo my first colonoscopy after he died, I cried when I arrived at the hospital. Medical procedures make me nervous. Having to endure one without Jay usually makes me miss him more and brings about a fresh tidal surge of grief. I quail at the idea of having to go through something like this without his comforting presence. Now I recognize that I need to rely on someone else as a supportive presence and not be stunned if a fresh round of grief surrounds this sort of experience for me.

Avoid comparisons with other survivors.

Don't get caught up in comparisons about your healing and grief journey with others. Everyone grieves in their own way and at their own pace. Healing from grief isn't a competition. By all means, don't feel guilty if you experience some relief or feel better than someone else. At the same time, don't get down on yourself for having a bad day. Try to keep your expectations for healing realistic. This journey can take several years and often, the greater the loss, the longer the passage.

Do something novel.

The aftermath of loss is a ripe time to acquire a new interest, hobby, skill, and/or friends. Changing your habits and routines can also be helpful. Take time to write out an individual mission statement for your life. Address what you value, what you stand for, and how you want to be known. The Buddhists refer to this as your *dharma*: Rick Warren calls it your *purpose-driven life*.[44] This written statement, which might begin with fits and starts, will evolve over time and provide a compass for a new direction.

Share your story.

Holding all your sadness inside yourself isn't good for your well-being, so consider expressive outlets such as talking, drawing, music, or writing about your experiences; expressive outlets augment healing. Some of the most important works of art, literature, and musical scores were created after periods of profound loss. It's important to tell your story of loss immediately and for some time thereafter. Sharing your story is what moves the healing process forward. Suzanne Hughes, a couples and family therapist in San Carlos, California, has created a specific writing project for grief survivors called Lost and Found.[45] She recommends the following guidelines for grief survivors to include in their story:

a. Write about what you lost and how you lost it.
b. Write about what you found from this loss and how you found it—this may not be "positive."
c. Write in the first person and write from your heart.
d. Include something about some gift you received from the situation or person you lost.

Identify what motivates you.

On your worst days, think long and hard about what motivates you to heal from loss. For me, it's always been our daughters, who themselves suffered greatly after Jay's passing. I didn't want my suffering to make theirs worse, and their presence in my life encouraged me to focus on my well-being. Bad days are also good times to turn to distractions: activities that give you a respite from active grief or encourage a sense of peace. A yoga, Pilates, or Zumba class works well, as does reading a stimulating or inspirational article or book. Julia Cameron describes the practice of *touchstones* for developing motivation.[46] This involves making a list of twenty-five things you love, and selecting one item each day that you access in some way.

Develop and use resources.

Develop resources and use them as necessary. I put together a team of resources—mostly people—but places, experiences, and information as well. For example, a massage therapist helped me experience regular physical touch. My acupuncturist and family doctor were also on my resource team. So was my yoga teacher, a financial adviser, and my trainers at the gym. I reached out for other resources, including a church, a meditation group, a Reiki worker, and a Vedic astrologer. Medication can be a resource, but it's not for everyone due to potential side effects.

Because I owned a large house and was inexperienced in aspects of home maintenance, I acquired resources to help me with home repairs and yard work as well. Sometimes unexpected places and people showed up on my resource team. Several months after Jay passed, I got a notice from the federal government indicating that I was entitled to a $250 death benefit. Because this wasn't a large sum of money, I procrastinated about visiting my local Social Security office. What a mistake. I should have gone there first. I'll never ever forget the kind woman who met with me and informed me I was also entitled to survivor benefits from Jay's Social Security funds. I was struggling financially, and this was the best news I received after his passing. The death of a family member almost always results in some kind of financial change—for better or worse—and consulting with a trusted banker, accountant, or adviser is an essential part of our well-being.

Counseling, including individual grief counseling and/or a grief support group, is an important resource for many people confronting loss. Several clients reported finding solace in support groups, surrounded by people who really got their experience. There are different kinds of grief support groups, including faith-based and secular. A particular issue that comes up for some individuals is the "God talk." Rebecca Hensler started an online support group for bereaved parents known as *The Compassionate Friends*, after realizing that the ones she'd attended were filled with large doses of spiritual language and religious and/or New Age interpretations.[47] Because she's an atheist, she found those groups problematic for her. You can find more information about her project at: http://www.griefbeyondbelief.org/.

Online support groups can be lifesavers for those with limited financial resources, but many practitioners adjust their fees for individual counseling based on a client's ability to pay. The Affordable Care Act, although under assault now, has made health care more accessible to a number of impoverished Americans. Some resources such as massage-therapy schools offer a number of services available for little to no cost from student providers. And the Bill and Melinda Gates Foundation offers financial resources for those with limited incomes through a program called Financial Services for the Poor. Financial stress makes grief worse so finding cost-effective, usable resources can be a game changer!

Some persons have a really hard time with healing and continue to feel extremely sad for a long time after the loss. About 7 percent of bereaved persons experience *complicated grief*, characterized by enduring sorrow, yearning, preoccupying thoughts of the loss, lack of acceptance of the loss; in effect, unrelenting sadness that persists so long it can be a serious health risk. In such situations, the Center for Compli-cated Grief at Columbia University recommends professional treatment that involves a series of structured weekly sessions relying heavily on cognitive behavioral therapy interventions such as grief monitoring and prolonged exposure and specific homework activities.[48] Dr. Katherine Shear, the director of this center, has presented empirical data underly-ing this approach in an article in the *JAMA Psychiatry Journal*.[49] You can contact the Center for Complicated Grief or the Association of Death Education Counselors at adec.org for trained grief professionals in your geographic area. The overall aim of complicated grief treatment is to help survivors maintain their connection with the lost person and begin to invest in the future simultaneously. While some survivors who have lost a child or someone to violence may be more at risk for compli-cated grief, no one is exempt from the possibility of struggling in such a way that their grief becomes protracted. Even persons who have lost something very precious and important such as a marriage or a coveted job may suffer from complicated grief as well.

In addition to complicated grief, over time, grief survivors also can encounter *cumulative grief*. As I was wrapping up this book, my only sibling and older sister, Peggy, died. It wasn't totally unexpected. She'd been in poor health for years and had shooed the angel of death away multiple times before. But not this time. I managed to get to Illinois, where she lived, before she passed away and had plenty of time to watch her try to die, a process compared to a woman being in labor giving birth. I was surrounded by her husband and their three adult children and had rich opportunities to talk with them about what might follow her death. I was sad but composed. I returned home and was immediately confronted with playing catch-up after being away for two weeks.

When I saw my acupuncturist that week and she asked, "How are you doing?" out of my body came "Sad," followed by large, heaving sobs. I cried the rest of the day. Because it was January, I was not only sad about my sister, but about Jay, my mom, and my dog, all of whom managed to choose January as their exit month. It puzzled me. I hadn't felt this sad in a long time. My usual optimism was out of reach. Finally, it dawned on me. I was experiencing the phenomenon known as cumu-lative grief. January is now a month of grief overload for me.

Cumulative grief has a snowball effect. A new loss builds on the prior loss(es) and in some way reignites the pain, much like the reopening of a wound that has been held together with very fragile stitches. Losses you believed you'd grieved successfully come back in a haunting fashion. The anniversary of a prior loss, or the anticipation of a future loss, all reemerge, often overwhelming you with sorrow and even shame. After all, your friends and family moved off the topic of grief long before you did. But if cumulative grief is left unprocessed, it raises the risk for complicated grief. Self-care is especially important when in the grips of cumulative grief. It's also important to reach out to others for additional support. Disenfranchised grief and ambiguous loss also may require special self-care and additional support resources. Disenfranchised grief occurs when there is a lack of societal acknowledgment or validation for the loss such as a death by suicide, HIV, drug overdose, or of a same-sex partner. Ambiguous loss involves unresolved grief that has no closure such as losing a beloved to dementia or losing someone who vanishes and doesn't return.

Recognize the potential transformational energies from loss.

Effective coping with grief is not about closure, but about using the loss as a life-changing experience. I agree with Max Strom that grief brings unexpected gifts, notably clarity, vision, and open-heartedness.[50] Stephen Jenkinson, interviewed in *The Sun* by Erik Hoffner, reminds us it's in the awareness of loss and death that we come to live more fully in the time we have left here on earth.[51] He speaks of grief as a teacher that helps us discern what's meaningful, what has value, and what can be discarded.

Grief teaches us about the importance of living life fully and completely and not taking anything for granted. Loss helps us recognize that life as we know it can change in a heartbeat or a breath. Loss is a wakeup call. Instead of moving ahead on automatic pilot, loss helps us reevaluate our past and current choices and make better decisions for the road ahead with new clarity and vision.

Cultivate a relationship with yourself.

The biggest takeaway message from my grief journey is this: what are you left with after you lose something or someone so precious? *Yourself!* For me, the worst loss now would be to lose myself to a substance, a job, or another person. The greatest gift is to be present to myself and, in the words of James Altucher, to choose myself.[52] This means remembering who I am and staying true to myself despite other persons or situations who expect me to do or be otherwise. Julia Cameron observes that often our greatest sense of loneliness and isolation comes not from a lack of relationships with others, but rather a lack of a relationship with ourselves.[53] After Jay died, I stuck a Post-it note on my computer with the following Byron Katie quote: "Just keep coming home to yourself. You are the one you've been waiting for."[54]

This theme was reflected in the most recent dream I've had from Jay—synchronistically while writing this chapter! The dream was a welcome foreshadowing of myself and my future and a stark contrast to the initial "Going to Buffalo" dream I had soon after Jay's passing. In this dream, I'm standing at the helm of a large schooner along with my two daughters, ready to cast off. Jay is on the dock standing next to the boat, a rope in his hand that secures the large boat to land. Although I'm a small-boat sailor and know nothing about large schooners, I'm feeling confident to captain this big boat into the waters. Jay throws the line to me and says, *"You've got this, babe"* while I cast off, and he walks away into the sunshine and joins up with his deceased father, mother, and sister as I sail off at the boat's wheel.

10

RESPONDING TO LOSS: GRIEF HELPERS

When we honestly ask ourselves which person in our lives means the most to us we often find that it is those who, instead of giving advice, solutions, or cures, have chosen rather to share our pain and touch our wounds with a warm and tender hand.[1]
—Henri J. M. Nouwen

Several months after Jay's death, a woman I barely knew came to my house and upon entering, burst into sobs. Gulping back tears, as her chest heaved, she said: *"I heard your husband died. I'm so sorry. I kept postponing paying my respects because I knew it would make me sad. My husband died about four years ago—very suddenly—and I have to tell you, grief doesn't get any better with time, it just gets worse!"* My heart weighed heavy seeing the intensity of her feelings and my hope for healing diminished.

I encountered a range of responses after Jay died. As the initial story illustrates, fellow grief survivors are not always the best grief helpers if their own grief is unprocessed. Obviously, the depths of this woman's pain took me away from my sadness and caused the focus of our interaction to shift to her. Some other responses I received felt very callous: *"Oh Sherry, get a grip. You're a strong person. You'll be just fine."* How did *she* know I would be fine?

How *do* we comfort and respond to someone who's had a major loss? We don't always know what to say or do. Sometimes this discomfort is due to survivors' guilt. We still have our good job or beautiful house so feel unsure about how to approach our neighbor who just lost his fifth job or our friend whose house went into foreclosure. We want to show care but we don't know exactly what to do or say that is helpful: *"Oh there have to be many people comforting Sherry. I don't know what to say to her so I won't deal with it right now,"* all the while hoping they don't run into me at the store. In our awkwardness over loss, we often retreat into silence, and that only makes the bereaved feel more alone and isolated.

Facing someone who has lost a loved one makes us have to stare death in the face, and that's uncomfortable. Stephen Jenkinson, author of *Die Wise,* believes particularly in US culture we suffer from *"grief illiteracy."* In an article written by Erik Hoffner published in *The Sun,* Jenkinson explains: "We have no language for what really happens, no ability to be a faithful witness, to do justice to how it feels to be dying in our time and place."[2] He describes our reactions to grief as impoverished.

How can we be effective grief helpers, particularly when our own experience with grief is either very limited or so overwhelming we are still processing it emotionally? In this chapter, I offer a number of guidelines. Rather than making you feel more self-conscious about responding to loss, I hope these suggestions sensitize you to typical things we say or do that arise from our own discomfort, inexperience, or obliviousness that inadvertently may cause the griever to feel worse. Even with sensitivity and guidelines, we won't always get it right!

How Can Our Words Help?

What can we say to a bereaved friend or family member? Phrases and intentions that *acknowledge* the situation are possibilities: *"I'm really sorry," "I wish things were different," "I imagine this is a hard time for you,"* or *"I'm thinking of you at this time."* Open-ended questions in which we do not presume the answer are also useful: *"What do you need now?"* or *"How can I best support you at this time?"* Owning our vulnerabilities is also useful: *"I wish there was something I could say or do to help at this time but I'm not sure exactly what that would be."*

How Do We Anticipate Needs?

Megan Devine, a social worker, writes in the Huffington Post of learning about grief firsthand when her partner drowned.[3] Not textbook grief about how to respond to bereaved clients, but firsthand-knowing-it-for-yourself grief. She provides recommendations for persons struggling with uncertainty about how, when, and where to respond. For example, she reminds us that grief belongs to the griever. Let the bereaved person take the lead and don't impose what you think should be done. She also recommends anticipating, not asking. Grief saps energy so don't ask the person to call you. Instead pick up the phone and make a concrete offer to help: *"I could pick up those clothes you need from the cleaners."* Also writing in the Huffington Post, Melanie DeSimone, coping with the loss of her son, has listed thirty-one practical and timely things to do for grieving families.[4] Her suggestions are amazing and include such ideas as colleagues donating sick and paid leave days, giving miles or points for travel, setting up an account for donations if needed, offering a spare guest room for out-of-town family, contributing a retreat space for private time, and offering to chauffeur as needed.

After Jay died, many folks said to me, *"Give us a call when you want to stop by."* It rarely happened. The grief helpers need to assume the responsibility for calling and initiating a plan because the bereaved don't have the energy to seek out the assistance we need. Helping with recurrent responsibilities such as walking the dog, shoveling the drive, mowing the grass, and weeding the garden are examples of useful acts. Devine cautions not to perform any task that is irreversible like laundry or cleaning because there may be something in the laundry or left around the house belonging to the deceased. Eliminating it could be a disaster.

How Does Our Presence Help?

Rev. T. McKinley writing in TheMighty.com suggests that we can't say anything to make someone's pain go away, but we can hold space for them and be fully present.[5] One of his suggestions for being a helpful presence is to simply invite them to tell you the story of their loss. And when they are finished with the telling, thank them for trusting you enough to share it.

Showing up as a helpful presence is also important on particular trigger days. Anniversaries of the date of the loss, birthdays, and holidays are difficult days for grievers. Track these days by putting them on your calendar as a reminder. Offer to do something with the person on such a day. Ask them to join you for a meal or see if they propose an activity. Be supportive in any way you can. Mention that you are thinking of the one they lost and follow up after that challenging day to see how they are faring.

How Can We Comfort?

Val Walker, author of *The Art of Comforting*, observes that there are skills involved in comforting others but so often we don't learn them.[6] Comfort, meaning "to be strong *with*," is an art form that has to do as much with our own unresolved issues (discomfort) around loss as it does with finding appropriate ways to respond. It's not uncommon for grief helpers to have unfinished feelings about loss become activated while trying to respond to someone else's emotional pain and sadness. When this prevents us from responding, or causes us to respond inappropriately, it's a clue *we* need some healing. Talking with a trusted colleague or friend often helps us process our feelings so we don't unload them inappropriately on someone else. In the moment, we can deal with our feelings by remembering to breathe, get grounded in the present moment, and focus on an image or thought that makes us feel safe. Francis Weller reminds us that we all carry some heartbreak within us—it may be a personal one or some sorrow about something happening in the world.[7] As Weller suggests, if we practice sharing our sorrows with each other by speaking honestly with at least one other person about the heartaches we guard so closely, our comfort with ourselves and others in grief and sorrow is greatly enhanced.[8]

How Do Cultural, Ethnic, and Religious Affiliations Impact Grief and Mourning?

Particular cultural/ethnic and religious groups may have beliefs and rituals for grieving that are unfamiliar to you. While Christians may have funerals or memorial services with music and assistance of church members, Roman Catholic Christian rituals involve a sacrament by the priest, a wake, a rosary, and a Mass of Christian Burial. Jewish mourners have specific observances that involve sitting "shiva" for seven days following the burial of the body and a period of official mourning lasts for one year. In the Islamic tradition, mourners are joined by family and friends for seven days.

In European American cultural groups, use of a funeral home or a clergy is prominent, as is a visitation at a funeral home with a social gathering following a service or internment. For many African Americans, their deep faith is almost always expressed in a church observance, sometimes called a "Home-Going" service. There is significant involvement with family, friends, and neighbors in the mourning process. Hispanic Americans typically rely on the services of a priest who conducts a Mass and says the rosary. Family and friends are an important part of bereavement.

Contrast this with Native American culture where the service is often moderated by a medicine man and one's ancestors are called in. Closely connected to nature, mourning includes nature representations of the deceased's "spirit." In many Asian American cultures, depending on the religious affiliation, the community elders are heavily involved in the service and mourning of the deceased, which also includes emphasis on the funeral route, choice of burial location, and some kind of monument marking the grave. Survivors create some kind of a shrine in their personal space to commemorate their dead loved one.

Part of effective responses to grief involves familiarizing yourself with the cultural practices that may impact the grief survivor you are helping.

Some Specific Recommendations for Responding to Grief Survivors

What ensues is a compilation of recommendations from the professional literature as well as personal observations and therapeutic work with grief-stricken clients for responding to loss. Again, rather than intimidating you with a number of right or wrong "rules" that increase your "performance anxiety," please view these as general guidelines that help you develop mindfulness about your responses to someone's grief. I admit that grief was a powerful teacher for me. Prior to losing my dad,

husband, mom, dog, and sister, I, too, often felt unsure about responding to a grieving person.

Prepare yourself.

Before approaching the person, consider that their world has been
rocked while our world is going on as usual. Be cognizant that their
sense of equilibrium has vanished. Don't be surprised by any of their
reactions—tears, sobs, stoicism, anger, bitterness, or even silence. They
may want to explode in anger or they may be shut down in shock. Don't
expect someone's level of grief to be based on the type of loss endured.
Someone who has lost a family pet or a very dear friend may grieve just
as intensely or as long as someone who lost a child or spouse. There's no
rating scale for grief.

Reach out in person.

Computers and smartphones are great but don't replace person-to-
person contact. Never text someone condolences. Emailing is not much
better. Phoning and leaving a message without an expectation for a
return call is useful and follow-up emails and texts are better received
after initial contact is made by phone or in person. It's wise to ask if they
want a visit rather than stopping by unannounced. If there's a Facebook
wall, posts on that, particularly those that share a memory, are helpful.
But don't post someone's status on your Facebook page unless they
have shared it on theirs. Allow them to take the lead on social media.

Leave the "fixing" alone.

Whatever their reaction is, remember we CANNOT FIX IT! We try
to fix someone because that makes US feel better. In our discomfort,
we want to provide a quick fix and then escape as if we are involved in a
"hit and run." It's not our job to fix or take away another person's pain.
We are just there to be a healing presence. A healing presence means
we act and speak in ways that have a positive impact on the other
person. Bereaved people don't need or want fixing, problem solving, or
advice. They benefit from comfort and support. Frank Ostaseski says
too often in serving those who grieve, we emphasize our role, not our
soul, and in doing so, set ourselves apart from their pain.[9] He believes
we get stuck in tasks or problem solving and lead with our tools instead
of our humanity.

Lose your expectations.

Don't expect ANYTHING from this person! Have a conversation, make a phone call, ask them to dinner, but don't expect something. They are struggling to hold it together and the last thing they deserve is our neediness. Don't make assumptions about how they're doing based just on outer appearance—they may look like a movie star but be racked inside with pain. They may appear uncharacteristically unkempt but feel peaceful on the inside.

Avoid platitudes.

Don't offer platitudes or false words of comfort. Don't say things like *"I know how you feel,"* or *"Your _____ is in a better place now,"* or *"This was God's will."* Don't advise them about what they can feel good about, or tell them it's time to move on, or ask if they've made strides on *"getting over"* their loss. Avoid all *"shoulds."* Don't ask, *"What happened?"* or *"How are you doing?"* They may not want to discuss what happened. They may not know how they are doing or may be weary of being asked that continually! Finally, don't use the interaction to tell them about your loss. This is about them and their loss.

Become comfortable with emotionally charged words.

Become comfortable with words like *death* and *dying.* Don't be afraid to use the word "death" in a conversation with them and also use the name of the deceased person liberally. *"Sherry, I'm so sorry that Jay died. Jay was such a terrific person and he died too young."* When we continue to mention the loved one's name even over time, it usually makes the survivor's heart sing, knowing that their loved one lives on in others' memories too.

Take cues from the griever.

Grievers provide verbal and nonverbal cues during interactions that signal their level of comfort. Learn to notice and follow these signals. While many folks heal by talking about the loss over and over, not everyone chooses to talk about it. Some may want to talk incessantly and others may not want to discuss what's happened—or may want to talk about something completely different as a way to take their mind off the subject. Don't assume what *we* want is what the bereaved wants. If unsure about cues, check it out: *"Maria, how could I be most helpful during our visit today?"* And as long as someone chooses to share their grief and pain with you, don't ever change the subject—that is equivalent to "pushing that person away."[10]

Offer support.

Ask *"What can I do?"* or *"Can I be helpful with _____ ?"* Be practical. Offer to run errands, walk the dog, or pick up food and drop it off. Most importantly, continue to be supportive for the long haul. Responding to someone's loss is not a short walk around the block; it's a long hike in the woods. Remember there's no timetable for grief. Some people suffer grief episodes for many years after a loss. Often the second or third year following a loss can be more challenging than the first. One of the worst things to do is to be present in the initial aftermath and then disappear.

Don't ever pressure a grieving person for a response to your offer of support and don't take a lack of one personally. Walker points out that some distressed persons resist support and comfort for fear of appearing too needy or vulnerable.[11] I don't believe as a griever I was alone in wanting to appear strong rather than weak after Jay died; at some level, I suspect many of us feel a sense of shame about our neediness and attempt to mask it.

Follow through on what you offer.

Take the initiative to be helpful but make sure you can really do what you offer. Assess your stamina, time, and resources. Offer to be there in ways that are consistent with your energy and availability. Above all, don't offer to do something and not deliver. This person is already consumed with disappointment so they don't need to be disappointed or abandoned by you as well.

Think carefully about tangible things to provide.

I don't recommend automatically bringing food or sending flowers just because someone is grieving. They may be inundated with food and have to throw it away. Flowers have to be disposed of in some way. Both of these gifts can create burdens for the bereaved at a time when they are already weighed down by sadness and additional responsibilities. A great gift I received was a spa gift card (notably provided by my awesome doctoral students!). After being a caregiver, or after losing someone precious, having something that nourishes you is amazing. Gifts given in memory of the loved one are meaningful. My neighbor, knowing how much Jay and I loved redbud trees, bought one in memory of Jay for our backyard and secured someone to plant it. Walker has a comprehensive list of comfort objects, movies, music, and books in her appendix that represents suitable symbolic gifts for bereaved persons.[12]

Ask directly about hard days.

Ask directly about their toughest times and if there are ways to help. For me, work days were manageable, but weekends, when I was accustomed to being with Jay, were terrible. I was consumed with loneliness. Walker suggests exploring not only the toughest times but also what makes them hopeful and keeps them going during the dark moments.[13] Does the memory of the loved one or the anticipation of a relative's phone call or knowing they are engaged in some meaningful life activity or something else encourage them to hang on despite awful circumstances or odds?

Be alert to cues of despondency and hopelessness.

Bereavement can raise the risk for suicide and this risk can increase around the anniversary of the loss. If there's any hint or threat the bereaved person's life is in danger, take this seriously and don't try to handle it without professional help.

In an Ideal World . . .

Following the loss of Jay, I wanted enough time and space to grieve without feeling the pressure of looking socially acceptable. In my situation, being composed was a burden I put on myself because I lived in a small town where I was known by many people, including current and former clients. At the same time, I was desperately lonely, especially around dinnertime and on weekends. Friends contacted me periodically, yet I often felt as if the responsibility for reaching out was on my shoulders. Although I had several friends who were conscientious about inviting me out, one thing I longed for was inclusion as a regular in couple and family dinners. Sometimes I'd cringe reading Facebook posts of my still-coupled friends about the things they were doing with each other. Many times I would run into couples and families at a restaurant or an event I attended solo and simply felt resentful, left out, and alone.

Responding to loss is a balancing act. How do we give someone who is grieving the space to heal and also be responsive to their needs? We reach out, ask, listen, and then respond accordingly, being a witness and comforting presence on their journey toward wholeness. Be the kind of person *you* would want in the midst of feeling like some part of yourself was severed by loss.

11

HEALTH, HEALING, AND HOPE

It is never too late to begin creating the bodies we want, instead of the ones we mistakenly assume we are stuck with. [1]
—Deepak Chopra

I wrote this book for people recovering from various losses. However, because my husband died from stage IV cancer, I have particular interest in the prevention and treatment of cancer. I hope this chapter jolts and inspires you.

Cancer is an epidemic in the United States. Currently, about 40 percent of our population has cancer, and one out of every two men in the country will develop cancer in his lifetime. My friend Vicki just called me. She's distressed because she found out one of her close friends was diagnosed with leukemia.

Vicki said, "Sherry, I'm in shock. Justine has never been a sickly person. How can this be happening?"

I understood the feeling. I thought Jay was the healthiest, strongest person I knew until the day he was diagnosed with stage IV esophageal cancer. Seemingly very healthy people are developing cancer at an alarming rate. In the last fifteen years, esophageal cancer has risen by 600 percent among white men in their sixties living in the United States. Middle-aged men are also being hit hard by HPV cancer producing oropharyngeal tumors, often from exposures decades before.

Vicki wondered if I knew anyone with leukemia. I recalled my former colleague and the several years of severe job stress that preceded his diagnosis.

"Well," Vicki said, "Maria sure was under a huge amount of job stress up until the very day she recently retired."

Stress and Illness

Does stress alone cause cancer? Of course not. Does stress impact the body's immune response increasing the probability that cancer or some other illness may result? Of course it does. We saw in an earlier chapter that chronic stress shortens the telomere length, resulting in poorer health and a shorter lifespan. Chronic stress also can make blood vessels that feed tumors grow more rapidly. Stress also impacts gene expression and potentially carcinogenic DNA mutations.[2]

I've always believed my husband's demanding work schedule—totally self-imposed—but still creating stress and pressure, had a role in the development of his esophageal adenocarcinoma. As several of our friends said to me after his diagnosis, "Jay always pushed himself." So true.

Stress is an important factor in the etiology of illness. Stress is associated with more visits to physicians and also with more diagnosed illnesses.[3] Mark Mincolla suggests that stress delivers a "ripple effect" throughout the entire body.[4] While short-term stress may have different effects, chronic stress impacts the body's ability to regulate the inflammatory response. Chronic stress has been linked to a number of health conditions including heart disease, stroke, and immune system dysfunction. And, as Stanford stress researcher Robert Sapolsky points out, getting stress under control doesn't *just* mean less physical illness; it also means we become nicer to each other since stress erodes our capacity for human kindness, compassion, and empathy.[5]

Lifestyle Factors and Illness

In addition, lifestyle factors can increase the risk of certain cancers and other illnesses too.[6] Processed foods—leading to weight gain—smoking, alcohol use, and a sedentary lifestyle are huge factors that contribute to both chronic and terminal illnesses, cancer included. Jay was an active person with a sedentary job, and until he met me, he'd smoked a pipe for a number of years. He also loved his high-carb, sugar-laden foods that led to weight issues. Certainly we all know people who are chain smokers, obese, or alcoholics who don't develop cancer, but these kinds of behaviors do raise your risk of cancer, heart disease, diabetes, or something else.

Given these risks, it would seem natural for people to modify their behavior and move toward health rather than illness. But as my friend Joe observed about his fifty-year-old chain-smoking mom who no longer has the lung capacity to climb stairs, she doesn't seem to give a "rat's ass" about her deteriorating condition. Unfortunately, research tells us that simply knowing about the benefit of making a lifestyle change doesn't result in people self-initiating such behaviors. Moreover, many persons also have difficulty seeing the long-term negative effects of their behaviors. Laura Carstensen, a psychologist and founding director of the Stanford Center on Longevity, points out that most people say they want to live to be a hundred in good health, yet also admit to eating too much and not exercising. In her article in *Time*, she asserts that that longevity is the result of many positive habits accrued over a lifetime.[7] Hope, Carstensen says is great, but we can't reach old age on hope alone![8] A long, healthy life requires changes in the way we live.

Behaviors like smoking, sitting, overeating, and so on are also potential addictions, and addictive behaviors can be challenging to change. Also, lifestyle modifications are either easier or more difficult to change depending on self-esteem. When we value ourselves, we are more likely to choose lifestyle behaviors that support health. Ethnicity also plays an important role, leading several psychologists to conclude that a cookie-cutter approach to fostering health behavior change isn't really viable.[9]

Financial Resources

Another factor that influences our lifestyle choices is financial resources. Not everyone has the money to purchase organic foods, gym memberships, complementary medicine treatments like acupuncture, Reiki, and massage therapy, or even adequate health insurance. Sometimes community-based programs provide these services. Those with higher incomes are typically more privileged in terms of access to health-care services, both standard and complementary. And, in the United States, higher income is associated with greater longevity, part of the privilege associated with a higher socioeconomic level.[10]

Exposures

The risk of cancer rises with the level of the things to which we're exposed. When Jay was last admitted to the hospital a month before he died, the attending oncologist who reviewed his lung scans asked, "Has he been exposed to anything?" A simple question, yet one I found difficult to answer. What *hadn't* he been exposed to?

Jay's only sibling died from ovarian cancer several years after Jay's death. No prior relatives in their family had cancer. But Jay and his sister had spent a number of formative years in a particular area of West Virginia where the incidence of birth defects and cancer is higher than usual due to exposure to environmental toxins. Certainly, this is one kind of exposure impacting the current high rates of cancer. Air and water quality are important factors in health and illness.

Exposure to nicotine also is a factor in the development of cancer and other illnesses too—COPD and emphysema. Exposure to processed foods, chemicals, hormones, and pesticides in foods can impact the body as well. In his book *Anticancer*, David Servan-Schreiber, a physician diagnosed with cancer, describes in great detail the role of environmental and nutritional exposures that contribute to cancer.[11]

These are the relatively known exposure factors in the development of illness. Other lesser-known factors have to do with exposure to interpersonal conflict and internal stressors. Most of us have some exposure to conflict with others in work and familial settings. While conflict itself isn't problematic, continued exposure to *unresolved* conflict with a friend, coworker, or family member that persists over years can adversely impact cells.[12] As Servan-Schreiber notes, the white blood cells of the immune system are particularly susceptible to feelings of helplessness.[13] Often in prolonged unresolved interpersonal conflicts, helplessness ensues. To me, there's no substitute in life for simple kindness. Treating ourselves and one another with kindness goes a long way toward well-being. Exposing ourselves to prolonged anger and grudges is bad for our health and the well-being of those around us.

Social Relationships/Loneliness

Social support is an important factor in maintaining health, although the ways in which social support contributes to health and longevity vary with culture, religious affiliation, and ethnicity.[14] Loneliness is a risk factor for illness, perhaps because our perception of social isolation makes us feel unsafe and vulnerable, producing a range of physiological responses.[15] Loneliness makes chronic stress worse, which, as mentioned earlier, impacts gene expression.[16] While we don't need an avalanche of friends, we can mitigate stress and illness by having at *least* several close confidantes we can depend on. When spouses die, a primary reason why men fare more poorly than women is because the men have cultivated only their spouse as their primary confidante and companion whereas women are more likely to have friends who serve this function in addition to their spouse. Social support can help us become resilient in the face of challenging loss by providing us with a sense of safety and strength.[17]

However, it's important to surround ourselves with people and friends who are uplifting rather than with those who are downers. As Paula Pietromonaco and Nancy Collins point out, close relationships can be sources of stress as well as support, especially in terms of negativity and social rejection.[18] Negative interpersonal relationships can be harmful to your health in much the same way as sedentariness and obesity.[19] Chronic complainers, those with anger-management issues, or other forms of negative energy aren't good sources of social support over the long haul. Assess carefully the persons you hang out with, in close relationships, work settings, and so on. Do these people nourish or drain you?

Thoughts and Feelings

In addition, what we think and how we feel also impacts our cells. Our thoughts impact our brain wiring. Mincolla explains that neurological studies demonstrate that every thought we think is registered in a particular area of the brain.[20] Our brain programs what's repeated most frequently in our thoughts.[21] If our thoughts and inner dialogue are negative, our brain wires negatively. If our thoughts and self-talk are positive, our brains wire positively. If we think something like *I'm happy, healthy, and peaceful*, this resonates differently with the brain than if we think *I'm unhappy* or *I'm a loser*.

Jay would tell you that he became attached to certain ways of thinking and feeling that were counterproductive, particularly in terms of male shame or self-defectiveness. Brené Brown, who I believe has advanced the discussion of shame and gender more than any other psychologist, asserts that while women suffer from shame from not being able to do everything perfectly enough, men experience shame from not being strong enough; from perceived weakness and vulnerability.[22] Jay was quick to recognize that and, toward the latter stage of his life, found the "work" of Byron Katie to be an effective way to detach from negative thoughts and feelings. In the "work," Katie asserts that thoughts are harmless unless we believe them, and most of us do! According to Katie, it's not our thoughts per se but our *attachment* to what we think that creates suffering.[23]

Do I believe Jay would be alive today if he had been able to control some of these exposures in his life? I can't say with any certainty because we don't know the role of genetics in Jay's cancer. What I do know is that exposure to various toxins increases the oxidative stress in the body, which adversely impacts our cells. Limiting harmful exposures, both internal and external, goes a long way toward prevention of cancer and other illnesses. Turner, a researcher in the field of integrative oncology, observes that the state of a person's mind-body-spirit "plays a pivotal role in whether or not toxins get removed from the body speedily, viruses and bacteria are allowed to take root, genes mutate, or cells break down."[24]

Luck

Sometimes getting a cancer diagnosis is simply a matter of bad luck. I know plenty of folks who have done all the right things and still have died from cancer. In some instances, cancer diagnosis, treatment, and outcome is a matter of attentiveness and luck. My friend Kitty just called. Her doctor had ordered a lung scan due to a chronic cough. The scan came back. The lungs were fine, but the radiologist spotted something on her kidney that turned out to be a tumor. The scan for her cough saved her life. Pure luck. She had no symptoms of having a tumor on her kidney.

As you know from reading my story, I had a gut instinct the year before Jay was diagnosed with the esophageal tumor that something was off with him. Yet the routine bloodwork he completed six weeks before his cancer diagnosis was normal. He did exhibit a cough several months prior to his diagnosis, which we attributed to spring allergies. Had Jay gone to his physician with this complaint, perhaps an earlier cancer diagnosis would have ensued. But no amount of self-recrimination helps if you've been diagnosed with cancer, or any other illness for that matter. And I know of people who DID visit a physician for early symptoms but who, for various reasons, were not diagnosed with cancer until weeks and months later, giving the cancer time to root and expand.

Paying Attention to Our Bodies

We all have cancer cells in our bodies. Only at certain times and for certain individuals do such cells grow into tumors, usually when our immune systems can't eliminate them.[25] I recommend paying close attention to your body without becoming hypochondriacal. And don't feel like a wimp for scheduling an appointment with your doctor to discuss something that doesn't feel quite right. If you feel something is amiss in your body and your doctor minimizes it, get another physician or a second opinion. Discuss and inquire about relevant screenings. While screenings aren't perfect, I know too many people in their sixties and seventies with severe colon cancer because they were too afraid to have the recommended colonoscopy screening at age fifty. I was in that category too! I waited to have mine after age fifty and discovered that, like everyone says, it's a "nonevent." The prep IS the worst part! If you're a white man in your sixties living in in the United States or if you have a history of acid reflux disease, I would insist on an upper endoscopy screening. Thyroid cancer is also on the rise, so make sure you ask your physician to check your thyroid gland with palpitation and always ask for the thyroid guard with any dental X-rays. Mammograms, ultrasounds, thermography, and pap smears are also useful standard screenings for women after a certain age. Skin cancer screenings are useful for melanoma detection. At the same time, remember, *there's no definitive test for cancer* at this time.

Obtaining Additional Opinions

I recommend getting a second opinion after a cancer diagnosis, although a caveat is that two or more opinions can be confusing. Jay's initial diagnosis occurred at our local community hospital and we were referred to a surgeon at UPMC, ranked thirteenth in the country at that time. This felt reassuring to us. Even more comforting was the opinion there that Jay's cancer was most likely confined to the esophageal area with metastases to the lymph, but questionable spread to the lungs. Because Jay wasn't a candidate for surgery—nor therefore for cure— the plan was to have UPMC oversee his case and administer his scans, but for him to receive chemo at our local university teaching hospital. We were a bit perplexed when our attending oncologist at the local teaching hospital viewed his scans and discussed the cancer evident in his lungs.

Physicians are people and they have differing opinions, but in fact, his cancer had progressed to his lungs, which is what killed him six months later. As the attending said in our initial visit with him, "You can live without a lot of organs, but not without your lungs!"

In retrospect, I wish we had sought a third opinion at the outset. Do your research and identify the treatment and research centers that are best known for the type of cancer and seek consultation there. At the same time, don't underestimate the value and competence of other treating facilities. Despite Jay's death, perhaps there's nothing I'm more grateful for than the skill and compassion of the physicians at our local teaching hospital. Although it was a teaching hospital, the seasoned oncologists there had years of experience in treating cancer patients, and it showed.

Monitoring

Another suggestion I have following a cancer diagnosis is to monitor everything. You can't assume that just because someone is under the care of a doctor or a patient in a hospital, everything will be closely watched. Your loved one needs an advocate, and if that can't be you, hire someone, or use other family members or friends to help. Read every single test report, lab report, scan, and so on. If you don't know what something means, ask. Keep asking until you feel satisfied with the response. Doctors and hospitals miss things all the time.

As an example, six weeks prior to Jay's cancer diagnosis, he had a kidney stone removed by a urologist. Several weeks before this proce- dure, he was required to get a chest X-ray. I remember reading the X-ray report and noting it said there was some "pleural effusion" in his lungs. I had no idea what that meant and I wasn't worried or even curious about it. I figured this report was being read by the radiologist and several doctors, none of whom ever mentioned anything about it. Now I know that pleural effusion in the lungs is a sign of abnormal fluid buildup and can indicate a variety of conditions including congestive heart failure, pneumonia, and cancer. Had someone in the medical community picked up on this, perhaps Jay's cancer would have been diagnosed earlier, when other treatment options might have been possible.

Listening to Your Gut

Finally, trust your own instincts and wisdom. You know yourself and the patient better than any health-care professional does. Continue to assert your knowledge on behalf of yourself and the patient, especially when you feel unheard. Jay was admitted to UPMC in mid-December for a surgical procedure to improve his swallowing. Despite the fact that his scan there about six weeks earlier had shown no sign of any cancer cells, I felt as if he had taken a huge recent downturn and was beginning the process of dying. Nowhere around me in this busy and remarkable hospital could I find anyone to hear this concern. I finally sought out the nurse in charge of his case and told her what I thought. "Oh no," she dismissed me. "He's certainly not dying now."

I admit, compared to the end-stage process of some other patients on the ward, he probably didn't seem as if he was in bad shape. But I lived with him and noticed subtle changes that alarmed me. In fact, he died six weeks later. I didn't take this conversation with the nurse further. The fact that it was growing close to the holidays didn't help. Hospitals are human places and become consumed with holiday plans and parties. I was also concerned with managing the upcoming holidays at our house and trying to be present for my husband. But clearly, further conversations were needed with hospital staff. It would be useful for each patient to have a hospital advocate, although getting insurance companies to cover this would probably be most challenging.

Making Wise Choices

Roger Walsh, MD, asserts that in contemporary well-funded countries such as the United States, diseases like cancer, cardiovascular disease, obesity, and diabetes are strongly determined by lifestyle factors including smoking, physical activity, alcohol intake, and diet/nutrition. He states there is a "growing awareness that contemporary medicine needs to focus on lifestyle changes for primary prevention, for secondary prevention, and to empower patients' self-management of their own health."[26] Yet despite the known advantages of making lifestyle changes to foster health, some patients are unable or unwilling to make them. In addition, as Walsh notes, huge industries are "geared toward encouraging unhealthy choices."[27] Walsh concludes that wide-scale adoption of healthy lifestyle factors will probably necessitate broad-range interventions including education, public health, mental health, and even political systems.

I concur with his analysis. Systemic interventions can produce societal change. But for me, there's no greater impetus for watching what and how I eat, sleep, move, and think than the recollection of my hand on my beloved husband's back during the last month of his life, viscerally feeling the breath leaving his lungs little by little, bringing death closer and closer with each inhalation and exhalation. Death and dying used to be abstractions for me. No longer. We all begin to die the moment after we're born, but some of us are passively killing ourselves earlier than necessary by our daily choices, the effects of which accumulate over years. While each of us has certain genetic influences, we now know that we can prevent many illnesses by our choices of nutrition, activity, thoughts, and emotions, all of which can impact gene expression.

The root of the words *health* and *healing* means wholeness. In her best-selling book *Kitchen Table Wisdom*, Rachel Remen reminds us that death is the great teacher and possibly the great healer as well.[28] I believe Jay found healing in death because his journey with terminal cancer led him toward healing his mind, spirit, and soul, even as his physical body deteriorated. And for me, I have found both health and healing as a passenger in Jay's journey, for in his dying I have embraced the preciousness of life.

Caretake this moment. Immerse yourself in its particulars.

It is time to really live; to fully inhabit the situation you happen to be in now. You are not some disinterested bystander. [29]

    —*Epictetus*

EPILOGUE: JAY

Real is something that happens to you when you're really loved a
long time.[1]
—Margery Williams

No discussion of my healing would be complete without saying more
about the subject of my grief, my beloved husband, Jay Howard Fast.
Jay, like most of us, was a perfectly imperfect person. He could be
unflinchingly stubborn even when it was in his own best interest to
yield. Our marriage of seventeen-plus years certainly wasn't conflict-
free, but somehow we always found our way back to each other.

Jay was in a class all his own. Dark haired, a bit stocky but solid, with
a smile that lit up a room when he spoke, Jay had an exceptional
warmth about him that melted people who encountered him. Not just
me, but our friends, our collective daughters, his clients, his coworkers.
This was evident in the way he approached you and in his tone of voice.
Whenever I heard, "Hi, honey" from him on the phone or in the house,
I was completely disarmed. His voice had a slight drawl and he always
stretched out his vowels; it was certainly the sexiest male voice I've ever
heard! He was also irrepressible and had quite a sense of wonder and
childlike innocence about him. The first book Jay introduced me to,
which I'd missed in my childhood years, long on hard work and short on
play, was Margery Williams's *The Velveteen Rabbit*.[2] His friends and
coworkers will attest to his warmth, humor, and utter playfulness. Jay
was a very hard worker who also managed to keep things lively
wherever he went!

Jay was a consummate psychotherapist, one of the best I've known. His capacity for connecting with and for understanding clients was unparalleled. He was always in demand because he worked hard on behalf of his clients and they knew it. He believed in them wholeheartedly, even when they found it troublesome to believe in themselves. He had an acumen about clients I found remarkable. One day, we were having a conversation about clients who had issues with theft. He reflected, "I've noticed that when working with clients who steal things, they felt something was taken from them first." His insights into himself and others were often stunning. I recall one Sunday when he returned from a trip to visit his parents. Lying in bed together that evening, he mentioned a question he'd developed on the drive home: "*How would your life be different if you were less afraid and felt more deserving?*"

Jay was also a first-class romantic. He believed in love, romantic love at its core. One of his favorite lines, which he often reminded me of, was from *Bull Durham: I believe in long, slow, deep, soft, wet kisses that last three days.* He wrote so many little love letters and notes to me and bought me so many cards that our friends joked we should own stock in Hallmark (we didn't). Sometimes, when leaving work, I'd discover he'd driven by the university parking lot to leave a love note under my car's windshield. Other times there would be a card on the bed for me to find when I woke up, characteristically later than he did. Jay counted the months and years of our relationship by the number of full moons. Periodically, he would say to me, "*Honey, I love you so much. We've been together now for 107 full moons.*" By the time he passed away, we were up to almost 250 full moons from the inception of our relationship.

On our wedding day, because he knew I loved the color purple, he presented me with a bouquet of purple dendrobium orchids to carry as his bride. Dendrobium orchids are known as the flower of wisdom and beauty. Thereafter, on every anniversary, I received purple dendrobium orchids, and as the years of our marriage ensued, the number of stems grew as well. On my birthday each year, among many cards and gifts, he also gave me a dendrobium orchid plant. In November 2007, the last year he was alive on my birthday, sure enough, another beautiful purple dendrobium orchid plant arrived. That particular dendrobium lasted the longest of any he ever gave me—seven years after his death—

reblooming successively, as if the plant itself was a messenger of his unending love and devotion.

Jay was generous beyond a fault. One year, the community mental-health center laid off the entire outpatient staff a month before Christmas. As a member of this group, Jay was part of the layoffs. I told him not to worry about getting me anything for Christmas that year. I figured our focus would be on our adult daughters. So I was amazed when, on Christmas morning, I walked into the living room and found a new cruising bicycle planted by the tree, with a big red bow around the handlebars and a card with my name on it. Sure enough, my honey had somehow managed to scrape together enough money to buy me a new bike that year. The city of Morgantown had just completed miles of biking trails, and Jay was eager to have me accompany him on his bike rides, which he'd been doing solo. I still ride that bike to the beach in my current Maryland community, and the bike was the inspiration for many trail rides together, some in the spring looking at the Virginia bluebells nestled among the hills, some in the fall, taking in the red, coral, and yellow hues of the turning trees in West Virginia. Often, we biked to a hotel on the river on the weekend to stop for brunch or supper.

Jay was a resourceful guy. Even though we never had a lot of money, we always had enough to celebrate occasions in a big way. For many years, on our wedding anniversaries, we went to the beach that week, just the two of us. As we became empty nesters, we often just stayed in town and had a special anniversary dinner at a wonderful restaurant. It wasn't unusual for us to get there and discover Jay had been there earlier in the day to set up little surprises. On the last anniversary we celebrated prior to his death, when we arrived at the restaurant, I delighted in the bouquet of purple dendrobium orchids he had placed earlier on our reserved table. Jay had also left a special Chris Botti CD with the waiter, and when we arrived, the CD started playing for us so we could dance. He was full of little loving touches like these throughout our relationship, so there was much to miss after he died, but there also was much to savor in remembrance.

During the last month of his life, while in the inpatient hospice situation, Jay's caring and romanticism were still at work. He enlisted the help of one of our friends, who would purchase cards she brought in for him to go through and say "yay" or "nay." After he died, she had an entire store of cards which she presented me with that he'd selected during that last month of his life. He anticipated the depth of my grief and wanted to show me that he was still with me, even though his physical body was absent from my side. In November 2008, the first birthday I would spend without him, my friend called and said, "Sherry, I want to take you out to lunch this year on your birthday." We were blessed with a beautiful, warm, and sunny mid-November day, unusual for that time of year in West Virginia, enabling us to eat outside on the restaurant's lovely outdoor deck. As the lunch ensued, my friend reached down and handed me a large birthday bag. She explained, "This is a birthday gift, Sherry, but it's not from me. My gift is the lunch. This gift is from Jay." She continued, "Jay knew this would be a very tough day for you. He knew you would miss him terribly on your birthday and feel especially sad that he wasn't sitting at this table cele-brating it with you. So he asked me to purchase a birthday gift for you that I would give to you today from him."

My heart leaped. How well my husband knew me! And is there anything more loving, more wonderful, or more intimate than being known so well by your beloved? His favorite quote from *The Velveteen Rabbit* came to mind: "Real isn't how you are made," as the Skin Horse explained to the Rabbit. "No, it's something that happens to you when you're really loved a long time."[3]

With tears welling in my eyes and streaming down my cheeks, I slowly reached into the bag. I pulled out an exquisitely handmade silk scarf that I immediately put on to grace my neck and sweater. It wasn't lost on me that the color of the scarf was turquoise, which, in Native American tradition, represents connection, protection, good health, and longevity. Now, each time I place it around my neck, I feel Jay's arms wrap around me with love. And I wrap my arms back around him, keeping his memory alive in my body and soul.

During the time that Jay had cancer, if he couldn't sleep, he would get up for a while and read and often make notes on the computer, which I discovered in a file after he died. One of the notes he wrote was about the issue of control. He said:

"Interesting word . . . Most seem to want it . . . Many fear losing it . . . Some think it's an illusion . . . Others see control as a problem rather than a solution. Well, I think at best I have control of myself when I can direct my attention toward a truth about me. When I do not want to face a truth that is beyond the boundary of my self-acceptance, I will usually try to control others or a situation. The degree to which I can catch myself and redirect my attention back to my own truth is the extent to which I can reclaim control of myself. I am then in a position to be relieved of my need to control others or the situation. I have connected with my own truth, my own essence, my own deep source, my own power. And . . . I can then welcome myself Home."

Welcome Home, Honey. I love you and miss you. And most of all, I remember you.

CONTEMPLATIVE QUESTIONS

Chapter 1

How has your sense of yourself changed by a significant loss or event?

How has your journey evolved following a loss or devastating event?

Chapter 2

A wise person once said, "There's no good news or bad news— there's just news." What's your reaction to this statement based on your life experiences?

What reactions did you have when reading Friday's Laws in this chapter?

Chapter 3

Can you identify any predominant illusions you cling to? How does holding on to them help or hurt you?

How do you struggle or come to appreciate "loving what is"?

Chapter 4

When have you experienced a trauma, loss, or crisis that evoked "a fear greater than death itself" and how did you move from fear to trust?

What is an example of something rebirthed in you after a traumatic loss or event?

Chapter 5

What is your take on the statement that we are all spiritual beings having a human experience?

What are your views about the place and role of visitation dreams after a loved one has died?

Chapter 6

Have you witnessed posttraumatic growth in yourself—or someone else?

Discuss the role of social support and relationships with others in healing and growth.

Chapter 7

Explore times in your life when turbulent events proved to be a catalyst for new growth and opportunities.

How do you stay centered in the midst of a topsy-turvy world? Misfortune or traumatic loss?

Chapter 8

What makes you hold on to something or someone so strongly even when you intuit that letting go is the healthier option?

How can you balance caring for yourself while caring for others as well?

Chapter 9

How has loss challenged you to form new assumptions and different ways of explaining the world in a way that makes sense to you?

How would you describe the transformational impact of trauma and loss on your life?

Chapter 10

What makes it hard to be present to the suffering of others?

Discuss the notion that in the United States, we are phobic about grief and loss.

Chapter 11

How can trauma and loss create wholeness in your body, mind, and spirit? Create healing and hope?

If death is the great teacher, what are the most important lessons?

Epilogue

What makes you feel better when you are with people who, like the Velveteen Rabbit says, are real?

What's the legacy of your loss or challenging life event?

NOTES

PREFACE

1. Pema Chodron, *When Things Fall Apart: Heart Advice for Difficult Times* (Boston, MA: Shambhala Publications, 1997), 71.

I. INTRODUCTION AND LOSS OF THE FAIRY TALE

1. Carl Jung, *Memories, Dreams, Reflections* (Pantheon Books/Random House, 1963).

2. SENSE OF AN ENDING

1. Paul Friday, *Friday's Laws* (Pittsburgh, PA: Bradley Oak Publications, 1999), 27.
2. Reprinted by permission of Paul Friday, ibid.

3. THE VEIL OF ILLUSION

1. Eckhart Tolle, *A New Earth: Awakening to Your Life's Purpose* (New York: Penguin, 2005), 28.

2. American Psychological Association, "Resolution on Palliative Care and End-of-Life Issues and Justification," 2017, http://www.apa.org/about/policy/palliative-care-eol.aspx.

4. THE TRANSITION AND AFTERMATH

1. Margaret V. Savage, "Unpublished Poem Written by Sherry's Sister 02/19/1942–01/02/2017," 2006.
2. Byron Katie, *Loving What Is* (New York: Three Rivers Press, 2002), 3.
3. C. S. Lewis, *A Grief Observed* (New York: Harper and Row, 1961), 3.

5. MANIFESTATIONS OF THE SOUL FOLLOWING DEATH

1. Thich Nhat Hanh, *Fear: Essential Wisdom for Getting Through the Storm* (New York: Harper Collins, 2012).
2. Grubbs, *Bereavement Dreaming and the Individuating Soul* (Berwick, ME: Nicolas-Hays, Inc., 2004).
3. Ibid.
4. Joel Martin and Patricia Romanowski, *Love Beyond Life: The Healing Power of After-Death Communication.*
5. Carl Jung, *Memories, Dreams, Reflections* (Pantheon Books/Random House, 1963).
6. Martin and Romanowski, *Love Beyond Life: The Healing Power of After-Death Communication.*
7. Grubbs, *Bereavement Dreaming and the Individuating Soul*, 125.
8. Ted Andrews, *Animal-Speak* (St. Paul, MN: Llewellyn Publications, 1993).
9. Carl Jung, *The Collected Works of C. G. Jung: The Structure and Dynamics of the Psyche*, vol. 16 (Princeton, NJ: Princeton University Press, 1970).
10. David R. Hawkins, *Power vs. Force* (Carlsbad, CA: Hay House Publications, 1995).
11. Grubbs, *Bereavement Dreaming and the Individuating Soul.*
12. Martin and Romanowski, *Love Beyond Life: The Healing Power of After-Death Communication.*
13. Sharon Ehlers, *Grief Reiki* (Ferndale, WA: AlyBlue Media, 2016).
14. Deepak Chopra, *Life After Death* (New York: Harmony Books, 2006).
15. Martin and Romanowski, *Love Beyond Life: The Healing Power of After-Death Communication.*

16. Grubbs, *Bereavement Dreaming and the Individuating Soul*.

17. Stephen Levine, *A Year to Live: How to Live This Year as If It Were Your Last* (New York: Crown Publishing, 1997), 115.

18. C. C. Marcus, *House as a Mirror of Self: Exploring the Deeper Meaning of Home* (Newburyport, MA: Conari Press, 1995).

19. Grubbs, *Bereavement Dreaming and the Individuating Soul*.

20. Coleman Barks, trans., *The Essential Rumi* (New York: Harper Collins, 1995), 122.

21. Grubbs, *Bereavement Dreaming and the Individuating Soul*.

22. R. J. Furey, *The Joy of Kindness* (New York: Crossroad Publishers, 1993), 138.

23. Ibid., 36.

24. Nhat Hanh, *Fear: Essential Wisdom for Getting Through the Storm*.

25. Candace Pert, *Molecules of Emotion: The Science Behind Mind-Body Medicine* (New York: Touchstone, 1999).

26. Judy Tatelbaum, *The Courage to Grieve* (New York: Lippincott and Crowell, 1980), 9.

27. Nhat Hanh, *Fear: Essential Wisdom for Getting Through the Storm*.

6. STARTING OVER AND POSTTRAUMATIC GROWTH

1. Joseph Campbell, *Reflections on the Art of Living: A Joseph Campbell Collection*, edited by Diane Osbon (New York: Harper Collins, 1991).

2. Karen S. Rook and Susan T. Charles, "Close Social Ties and Health in Later Life: Strengths and Vulnerabilities," *The American Psychologist* 72, no. 6 (September 2017): 567–77.

3. John Norcross, *Changeology* (New York: Simon and Schuster, 2012).

4. Wallace Nichols, *Blue Mind* (New York: Little, Brown and Company, 2014).

5. Richard Tedeschi and Lawrence Calhoun, "The Posttraumatic Growth Inventory: Measuring the Positive Legacy of Trauma," *Journal of Traumatic Stress* 9, no. 3 (January 1, 1996): 455–71.

6. Stephen Joseph, *What Doesn't Kill Us: The New Psychology of Posttraumatic Growth* (New York: Basic Books, 2011).

7. Lawrence Calhoun and Richard Tedeschi, *Posttraumatic Growth in Clinical Practice* (New York: Routledge, 2013).

8. Richard Tedeschi and Bret Moore, *The Posttraumatic Growth Workbook: Coming through Trauma Wiser, Stronger, and More Resilient* (Oakland, CA: New Harbinger Publications, 2016).

9. Joseph, *What Doesn't Kill Us: The New Psychology of Posttraumatic Growth*.

10. Stephen Joseph, *Positive Psychology in Practice: Promoting Human Flourishing in Work, Health, Education, and Everyday Life*, second edition (Hoboken, NJ: Wiley, 2015).

11. Lawrence Calhoun and Richard Tedeschi, eds., *Handbook of Posttraumatic Growth: Research and Practice* (Mahwah, NJ: Lawrence Erlbaum Associates, 2006).

12. Calhoun and Tedeschi, *Posttraumatic Growth in Clinical Practice*, 19.

13. Kate Bower, *Everything Happens for a Reason* (New York: Random House, 2017).

14. Camille Wortman, "Posttraumatic Growth: Progress and Problems," *Psychological Inquiry* 15, no. 1 (2004): 81–90.

15. Laurie Pearlman, *Treating Traumatic Bereavement: A Practitioner's Guide* (New York: The Guilford Press, 2014).

16. Christine Schubert, Ulrike Schmidt, and Rita Rosner, "Posttraumatic Growth in Populations with Posttraumatic Stress Disorder—A Systematic Review on Growth-Related Psychological Constructs and Biological Variables," *Clinical Psychology and Psychotherapy* 23, no. 6 (November 2016): 469–86.

17. Joseph, *What Doesn't Kill Us: The New Psychology of Posttraumatic Growth*, 167.

18. Lorna Collier, "Growth After Trauma," *American Psychological Association* 47, no. 10 (2016): 48.

19. Frank J. Infurna et al., "Changes in Life Satisfaction When Losing One's Spouse: Individual Differences in Anticipation, Reaction, Adaptation and Longevity in the German Socio-Economic Panel Study (SOEP)," *Ageing and Society* 37, no. 5 (May 2017): 899–934.

7. TURBULENCE AND CHANGE

1. Margaret V. Savage, unpublished note, 2011.

2. Dennis Klass, Phyllis Silverman, and Steven Nickman, *Continuing Bonds* (Washington, DC: Taylor and Francis, 1996).

3. Melody Warnick, *This Is Where You Belong* (New York: Viking, 2016).

4. Ibid.

5. Meghan O'Rourke, "Good Grief," *The New Yorker*, January 25, 2010, https://www.newyorker.com/magazine/2010/02/01/good-grief.

6. C. Murray Parkes, "Determinants of Outcome Following Bereavement," *OMEGA–Journal of Death and Dying* 6, no. 4 (January 1, 1976): 303–23.

7. Warnick, *This Is Where You Belong*.

8. James Pennebaker, *Writing to Heal*, Oakland, CA: New Harbinger Publications, 2004.

9. Laura Oliver, *The Story Within: New Insights and Inspiration for Writers* (New York: Penguin, 2011).

10. Anne Lamott, *Daily Good: News That Inspires*, November 3, 2017, http://www.dailygood.org/story/1722/anne-lamott-author-writes-down-every-single-thing-she-knows-as-of-today-anne-lamott/.

11. Elisabeth Kübler-Ross, *On Death and Dying* (New York: Routledge, 1969).

8. LETTING GO AND FACING LOSS: STRESS AND SELF-CARE

1. Richard Miller, *Yoga Nidra: A Meditative Practice for Deep Relaxation and Healing* (Boulder, CO: Sounds True, 2005), 22.

2. Jim Rendon, *Upside: The New Science of Post-Traumatic Growth* (New York: Touchstone, 2015).

3. Elizabeth Blackburn and Elissa Epel, *The Telomere Effect* (New York: Grand Central Publishing, 2017).

4. Ibid.

5. Eleanor Law et al., "Telomeres and Stress: Promising Avenues for Research in Psycho-Oncology." *Asia-Pacific Journal of Oncology Nursing* 3, no. 2 (2016): 137–47; Stacy Lu, "How Chronic Stress Is Harming Our DNA," *Monitor on Psychology* 45, no. 9 (2014): 28; Scott Sleek, "The Long and the Short of It," *APS Observer* 27, no. 9 (October 31, 2014), https://www.psychologicalscience.org/observer/the-long-and-the-short-of-it.

6. Blackburn and Epel, *The Telomere Effect*.

7. Neal Lathia et al., "Happier People Live More Active Lives: Using Smartphones to Link Happiness and Physical Activity," *PLOS ONE* 12, no. 1 (January 4, 2017).

8. Katie Hafner, "Researchers Confront an Epidemic of Loneliness," *New York Times*, September 5, 2016, https://www.nytimes.com/2016/09/06/health/loneliness-aging-health-effects.html.

9. Rendon, *Upside: The New Science of Post-Traumatic Growth*.

10. Phyllis Silverman and Madelyn Kelly, *A Parent's Guide to Raising Grieving Children* (New York: Oxford University Press, 2009), 6.

11. Karen Rook and Susan Charles, "Close Social Ties and Health in Later Life: Strengths and Vulnerabilities," *The American Psychologist* 72, no. 6 (September 2017): 567–77.

12. Ruth Nemzoff, *Don't Bite Your Tongue: How to Foster Rewarding Relationships with Your Adult Children* (New York: St. Martin's Griffin, 2008).

13. Todd Kashdan, *Curious?* (New York: Harper Collins, 2009).

14. University of Wisconsin–Madison, "Science Overview—Center for Healthy Minds," 2017, https://centerhealthyminds.org/science/overview.

15. Richard Miller, *The iRest Program for Healing PTSD: A Proven Effective Approach to Using Yoga Nidra Meditation and Deep Relaxation to Overcome Trauma* (Oakland, CA: New Harbinger Publications, 2015).

16. Richard Miller, *Resting in Stillness* (San Rafael, CA: Integrative Restoration Institute, 2011).

17. Linda Graham, *Bouncing Back: Rewiring Your Brain for Maximum Resilience and Well-Being* (Novato, CA: New World Library, 2013).

18. Rendon, *Upside: The New Science of Post-Traumatic Growth.*

19. Kelly Turner, *Radical Remission* (New York: Harper Collins, 2004).

20. Pema Chodron, *When Things Fall Apart: Heart Advice for Difficult Times* (Boston, MA: Shambhala Publications, 1997).

21. Anne Lamott, "It's Been Said That Expectations Are Resentments under Construction," Facebook post, November 5, 2014.

22. Eckhart Tolle, *A New Earth: Awakening to Your Life's Purpose* (New York: Penguin, 2005).

23. Lawrence Calhoun and Richard Tedeschi, eds., *Handbook of Posttraumatic Growth: Research and Practice* (Mahwah, NJ: Lawrence Erlbaum Associates, 2006).

24. Ibid.

25. Dan McAdams, *The Redemptive Self* (New York: Oxford University Press, 2006).

26. Harold Kushner, *When Bad Things Happen to Good People* (New York: Schocken Books, a division of Random House, 1981).

27. Mark Nepo, *The Book of Awakening* (San Francisco, CA: Conari Press, 2011), 348.

28. Murray Bowen, *Family Therapy in Clinical Practice* (Lanham, MD: Jason Aronson, 1978).

29. Robert Firestone, Lisa A. Firestone, and Joyce Catlett, *The Self under Siege: Voice Therapy and Differentiation* (New York: Routledge, 2013).

30. Judith Viorst, *Necessary Losses* (New York: The Free Press, 1986).

9. COPING WITH LOSS: GRIEF SURVIVORS

1. Ernest Hemingway, *A Farewell to Arms* (New York: Scribner and Sons, 1929), 267.

2. Pauline Boss and Donna Carnes, "The Myth of Closure," *Family Process* 51, no. 4 (December 2012): 456–69.

3. Ibid.

4. Elizabeth Lesser, *Broken Open* (New York: Villard Books, 2005).

5. Dietrich Bonhoeffer, *A Year with Dietrich Bonhoeffer: Daily Meditations from His Letters, Writings, and Sermons*, first edition (San Francisco: HarperOne, 2005).

6. Ibid., 176.

7. Lesser, *Broken Open*.

8. Jill Bolte Taylor, *My Stroke of Insight* (New York: Viking, 2006).

9. Richard Davidson and Sharon Begley, *The Emotional Life of Your Brain* (New York: Penguin, 2012), xi.

10. Ibid.

11. Brendon Burchard, *High Performance Habits: How Extraordinary People Become That Way* (Carlsbad, CA: Hay House, 2017).

12. Frank J. Infurna and Suniya S. Luthar, "The Multidimensional Nature of Resilience to Spousal Loss," *Journal of Personality and Social Psychology* 112, no. 6 (2017): 926–47.

13. Mandy Oaklander, "Bounce Back," *Time*, June 1, 2015.

14. Daniel Goleman and Richard Davidson, *Altered Traits: Science Reveals How Meditation Changes Your Mind, Brain, and Body* (New York: Avery Books, 2017).

15. Sherilyn L. Cormier, Paula Nurius, and Cynthia J. Osborn, *Interviewing and Change Strategies for Helpers*, seventh edition (Belmont, CA: Brooks/Cole, Cengage Learning, 2013), 472.

16. Jon Kabat-Zinn, "Mindfulness Meditation—Guided Mindfulness Meditation Practices with Jon Kabat-Zinn," 2017, https://www.mindfulnesscds.com/; Jon Kabat-Zinn, "Mindfulness Apps with Jon Kabat-Zinn," 2017, http://mindfulnessapps.com/.

17. Jon Kabat-Zinn, *Mindfulness for Beginners* (Boulder, CO: Sounds True, 2012).

18. Elizabeth A. Hoge, Eric Bui, Sophie A. Palitz, Noah R. Schwarz, Maryann E. Owens, Jennifer M. Johnston, Mark H. Pollack, and Naomi M. Simon, "The Effect of Mindfulness Meditation Training on Biological Acute Stress Responses in Generalized Anxiety Disorder," *Psychiatry Research*, January 25, 2017; J. David Creswell, "Mindfulness Interventions," *Annual Review of Psychology* 68 (2017): 491–516.

19. Davidson and Begley, *The Emotional Life of Your Brain*.

20. Boss and Carnes, "The Myth of Closure."

21. Infurna and Luthar, "The Multidimensional Nature of Resilience to Spousal Loss."

22. Davidson and Begley, *The Emotional Life of Your Brain*.

23. Susan David, *Emotional Agility* (New York: Avery, 2016).

24. Boss and Carnes, "The Myth of Closure."

25. King, Heintzelman, and Ward, "Beyond the Search for Meaning."

26. Chelsea Avery, "The New Wifestyle: Empowering Women and Our Relationships," https://thenewwifestyle.com/tag/the-new-wifestyle-blog/.

27. Kira Newman, "Five Science-Based Strategies for More Happiness," *Greater Good Science Center*, March 16, 2016.

28. Davidson and Begley, *The Emotional Life of Your Brain*.

29. Laura A. King, Samantha J. Heintzelman, and Sarah J. Ward, "Beyond the Search for Meaning: A Contemporary Science of the Experience of Meaning in Life," *Current Directions in Psychological Science* 25, no. 4 (August 1, 2016): 211–16.

30. Amy Gallo, "How to Turn a Bad Day Around," *Harvard Business Review*, October 16, 2015.

31. Shawn Achor, *The Happiness Advantage* (New York: Random House, 2010).

32. Mojo Creations, "Mojo. Fitness for the Soul," *Mojo Creations*, 2015, http://mojocreations.com/.

33. Alex M. Wood, Jeffrey J. Froh, and Adam W. A. Geraghty, "Gratitude and Well-Being: A Review and Theoretical Integration," *Clinical Psychology Review* 30, no. 7 (November 2010): 890–905.

34. Prathik Kini, Joel Wong, Sydney McInnis, Nicole Gabana, and Joshua W. Brown, "The Effects of Gratitude Expression on Neural Activity," *NeuroImage* 128 (March 2016): 1–10.

35. Paul J. Mills, Laura Redwine, Kathleen Wilson, Meredith A. Pung, Kelly Chinh, Barry H. Greenberg, Ottar Lunde, et al., "The Role of Gratitude in Spiritual Well-Being in Asymptomatic Heart Failure Patients," *Spirituality in Clinical Practice (Washington, D.C.)* 2, no. 1 (March 2015): 5–17.

36. Robert Emmons, *Gratitude Works!* (San Francisco, CA: Jossey-Bass, 2013).

37. Arthur C. Brooks, "Opinion: Choose to Be Grateful. It Will Make You Happier," *New York Times*, November 21, 2015.

38. Kini et al., "The Effects of Gratitude Expression on Neural Activity."

39. Alexandra Sifferlin, "The Healing Power of Nature," *Time*, July 13, 2016.

40. Ibid.

41. Gregory N. Bratman, J. Paul Hamilton, Kevin S. Hahn, Gretchen C. Daily, and James J. Gross, "Nature Experience Reduces Rumination and Subgenual Prefrontal Cortex Activation," *Proceedings of the National Academy of Sciences of the United States of America* 112, no. 28 (July 14, 2015): 8567–72.

42. Newman, "Five Science-Based Strategies for More Happiness."

43. Florence Williams, *The Nature Fix: Why Nature Makes Us Happier, Healthier, and More Creative*, first edition (New York: Norton, 2017).

44. Rick Warren, *The Purpose Driven Life* (Grand Rapids, MI: Zondervan, 2012).

45. Suzanne Hughes, "Project Lost and Found," *Project Lost and Found*, 2017, http://www.projectlostandfound.com/.

46. Julia Cameron, *It's Never Too Late to Begin Again* (New York: Tarcher/Perigee, 2016).

47. Rebecca Hensler, "Grief Beyond Belief," http://www.griefbeyondbelief.org/.

48. Columbia School of Social Work, "The Center for Complicated Grief—Grief Is a Form of Love," *The Center for Complicated Grief*, 2017, https://complicatedgrief.columbia.edu.

49. Katherine M. Shear, Charles F. Reynolds, Naomi M. Simon, Sidney Zisook, Yuanjia Wang, Christine Mauro, Naihua Duan, Barry Lebowitz, and Natalia Skritskaya, "Optimizing Treatment of Complicated Grief: A Randomized Clinical Trial," *JAMA Psychiatry* 73, no. 7 (July 1, 2016): 685–94.

50. Max Strom, *There Is No App for Happiness* (New York: Skyhorse Publishing, 2013).

51. Erik Hoffner, "As We Lay Dying: Stephen Jenkinson on How We Deny Our Mortality," *The Sun*, August 2015.

52. James Altucher, *Choose Yourself* (Austin, TX: Lioncrest Publishing, 2013).

53. Cameron, *It's Never Too Late to Begin Again*.

54. Byron Katie, *Loving What Is* (New York: Three Rivers Press, 2002), 312.

10. RESPONDING TO LOSS: GRIEF HELPERS

1. Henri J. M. Nouwen, *Out of Solitude* (Notre Dame, IN: Ave Maria Press, 2004), 38.

2. Erik Hoffner, "As We Lay Dying: Stephen Jenkinson on How We Deny Our Mortality," *The Sun Magazine*, August 2015, https://www.thesunmagazine.org/issues/476/as-we-lay-dying.

3. Megan Devine, "How to Help a Grieving Friend: 11 Things to Do When You're Not Sure What to Do," *Huffington Post*, November 25, 2013, https://www.huffingtonpost.com/megan-devine/death-and-dying_b_4329830.html.

4. Melanie DeSimone, "31 Practical Ways to Love Grieving Families in the First Few Days," *Huffington Post*, February 25, 2016, https://www.huffingtonpost.com/melanie-desimone/31-practical-ways-to-love-grieving-families-in-the-first-few-days_b_9193060.html.

5. T. McKinley, "There Is Nothing You Can Say to Heal Someone Else's Grief," *The Mighty*, December 5, 2016, https://themighty.com/2016/12/what-to-say-to-someone-whos-grieving/.

6. Val Walker, *The Art of Comforting* (New York: Tarcher/Penguin, 2010).

7. Francis Weller, *The Wild Edge of Sorrow* (Berkeley, CA: North Atlantic Books, 2015).

8. Ibid.

9. Frank Ostaseski, *The Five Invitations: Discovering What Death Can Teach Us About Living Fully*, first edition (New York: Flatiron Books, 2017).

10. Max Strom, *There Is No App for Happiness* (New York: Skyhorse Publishing, 2013).

11. Walker, *The Art of Comforting*.

12. Ibid.

13. Ibid.

11. HEALTH, HEALING, AND HOPE

1. Deepak Chopra, *Perfect Health: The Complete Mind/Body Guide* (New York: Harmony Books, 1994), 309.

2. Susan K. Lutgendorf and Barbara L. Andersen, "Biobehavioral Approaches to Cancer Progression and Survival: Mechanisms and Interventions," *The American Psychologist* 70, no. 2 (March 2015): 186–97.

3. Paul A. Pirraglia, John M. Hampton, Allison B. Rosen, and Whitney P. Witt, "Psychological Distress and Trends in Healthcare Expenditures and Outpatient Healthcare," *The American Journal of Managed Care* 17, no. 5 (May 2011): 319–28.

4. Mark Mincolla, *Whole Health* (New York: Tarcher/Penguin, 2013).

5. Robert Sapolsky, *Behave: The Biology of Humans at Our Best and Worst* (New York: Penguin Press, 2017).

6. Bonnie Spring, Abby C. King, Sherry L. Pagoto, Linda Van Horn, and Jeffery D. Fisher, "Fostering Multiple Healthy Lifestyle Behaviors for Primary Prevention of Cancer," *The American Psychologist* 70, no. 2 (March 2015): 75–90.

7. Laura Carstensen, "The New Age of Aging," *Time*, February 10, 2016.

8. Ibid.

9. Spring et al., "Fostering Multiple Healthy Lifestyle Behaviors for Primary Prevention of Cancer."

10. Raj Chetty, Michael Stepner, Sarah Abraham, Shelby Lin, Benjamin Scuderi, Nicholas Turner, Augustin Bergeron, and David Cutler, "The Association Between Income and Life Expectancy in the United States, 2001–2014," *JAMA* 315, no. 16 (April 26, 2016): 1750.

11. David Servan-Schreiber, *Anticancer* (New York: Penguin, 2008).

12. Ibid.

13. Ibid.

14. Belinda Campos and Heejung S. Kim, "Incorporating the Cultural Diversity of Family and Close Relationships into the Study of Health," *American Psychologist* 72, no. 6 (September 2017): 543–54.

15. Laura Carstensen, *A Long Bright Future : An Action Plan for a Lifetime of Happiness, Health, and Financial Security*, first edition (New York: Broadway Books, 2009).

16. Sapolsky, *Behave*.

17. Paula Pietromonaco and Nancy Collins, "Interpersonal Mechanisms Linking Close Relationships to Health," *The American Psychologist* 72, no. 6 (September 2017): 531–42.

18. Ibid.

19. Bert N. Uchino, Richard M. Cawthon, Timothy W. Smith, Kathleen C. Light, Justin McKenzie, McKenzie Carlisle, Heather Gunn, Wendy Birmingham, and Kimberly Bowen, "Social Relationships and Health: Is Feeling Positive, Negative, or Both (Ambivalent) about Your Social Ties Related to Telomeres?" *Health Psychology: Official Journal of the Division of Health Psychology, American Psychological Association* 31, no. 6 (November 2012): 789–96.

20. Mincolla, *Whole Health*.

21. Ibid.

22. Brené Brown, *Daring Greatly* (New York: Avery, 2012).

23. Byron Katie, *Loving What Is* (New York: Three Rivers Press, 2002).

24. Kelly Turner, *Radical Remission* (New York: Harper Collins, 2014), 280.

25. Ty Bollinger, *The Truth about Cancer* (Carlsbad, CA: Hay House Publications, 2016).

26. Roger Walsh, "Lifestyle and Mental Health," *The American Psychologist* 66, no. 7 (October 2011): 579.

27. Ibid., 588.

28. Rachel Remen, *Kitchen Table Wisdom* (New York: Riverhead Books, 1996).

29. Epictetus, *The Art of Living* (Charlotte, NC: Starr Publications, 2017), 113.

EPILOGUE: JAY

1. Margery Williams, *The Velveteen Rabbit* (New York: George H. Duran Co., 1922), 5.

2. Williams, *The Velveteen Rabbit*.

3. Ibid., 5.

BIBLIOGRAPHY

Achor, Shawn. *The Happiness Advantage*. New York: Random House, 2010.

Altucher, James. *Choose Yourself*. Austin: Lioncrest Publishing, 2013.

American Psychological Association. "Resolution on Palliative Care and End-of-Life Issues and Justification." *apa.org*, 2017. http://www.apa.org/about/policy/palliative-care-eol.aspx.

Andrews, Ted. *Animal-Speak*. St. Paul: Llewellyn Publications, 1993.

Avery, Chelsea. "The New Wifestyle: Empowering Women and Our Relationships." *The New Wifestyle*, 2017. https://thenewwifestyle.com/.

Barks, Coleman, trans. *The Essential Rumi*. New York: Harper Collins, 1995.

Blackburn, Elizabeth, and Elissa Epel. *The Telomere Effect*. New York: Grand Central Publishing, 2017.

Bollinger, Ty. *The Truth about Cancer*. Carlsbad, CA: Hay House Publications, 2016.

Bonhoeffer, Dietrich. *A Year with Dietrich Bonhoeffer: Daily Meditations from His Letters, Writings, and Sermons*. First edition. San Francisco: HarperOne, 2005.

Boss, Pauline. *Myth of Closure*. n.d. https://onbeing.org/programs/pauline-boss-the-myth-of-closure/ (accessed June 23, 2016).

Boss, Pauline, and Donna Carnes. "The Myth of Closure." *Family Process* 51, no. 4 (December 2012): 456–69. doi:10.1111/famp.12005.

Bowen, Murray. *Family Therapy in Clinical Practice*. Lanham, MD: Jason Aronson, 1978.

Bower, Kate. *Everything Happens for a Reason*. New York: Random House, 2017.

Bratman, Gregory N., J. Paul Hamilton, Kevin S. Hahn, Gretchen C. Daily, and James J. Gross. "Nature Experience Reduces Rumination and Subgenual Prefrontal Cortex Activation." *Proceedings of the National Academy of Sciences of the United States of America* 112, no. 28 (July 14, 2015): 8567–72. doi:10.1073/pnas.1510459112.

Brooks, Arthur C. "Opinion: Choose to Be Grateful. It Will Make You Happier." *New York Times*, November 21, 2015. https://www.nytimes.com/2015/11/22/opinion/sunday/choose-to-be-grateful-it-will-make-you-happier.html.

Brown, Brené. *Daring Greatly*. New York: Avery, 2012.

Burchard, Brendon. *High Performance Habits: How Extraordinary People Become That Way*. Carlsbad, CA: Hay House, 2017.

Calhoun, Lawrence G., and Richard G. Tedeschi, eds. *Handbook of Posttraumatic Growth: Research and Practice*. Mahwah, NJ: Lawrence Erlbaum Associates, 2006.

———. *Posttraumatic Growth in Clinical Practice*. New York: Routledge, 2013.

Cameron, Julia. *It's Never Too Late to Begin Again*. New York: Tarcher/Perigee, 2016.

Campbell, Joseph. *Reflections on the Art of Living: A Joseph Campbell Collection*. Edited by Diane Osbon. New York: Harper Collins, 1991.

Campos, Belinda, and Heejung S. Kim. "Incorporating the Cultural Diversity of Family and Close Relationships into the Study of Health." *American Psychologist* 72, no. 6 (September 2017): 543–54. doi:10.1037/amp0000122.

Carstensen, Laura. *A Long Bright Future: An Action Plan for a Lifetime of Happiness, Health, and Financial Security*. First edition. New York: Broadway Books, 2009.

———. "The New Age of Aging." *Time*, February 10, 2016.

Chetty, Raj, Michael Stepner, Sarah Abraham, Shelby Lin, Benjamin Scuderi, Nicholas Turner, Augustin Bergeron, and David Cutler. "The Association Between Income and Life Expectancy in the United States, 2001–2014." *JAMA* 315, no. 16 (April 26, 2016): 1750. doi:10.1001/jama.2016.4226.

Chodron, Pema. *When Things Fall Apart: Heart Advice for Difficult Times*. Boston: Shambhala Publications, 1997.

Chopra, Deepak. *Life After Death*. New York: Harmony Books, 2006.

———. *Perfect Health: The Complete Mind/Body Guide*. New York: Harmony Books, 1994.

Collier, Lorna. "Growth After Trauma." American Psychological Association 47, no. 10 (2016): 48.

Columbia School of Social Work. "The Center for Complicated Grief—Grief Is a Form of Love." *The Center for Complicated Grief*, 2017. https://complicatedgrief.columbia.edu.

Cormier, L. Sherilyn, Paula Nurius, and Cynthia J. Osborn. *Interviewing and Change Strategies for Helpers*. Seventh edition. Belmont, CA: Brooks/Cole, Cengage Learning, 2013.

Creswell, J. David. "Mindfulness Interventions." *Annual Review of Psychology* 68 (2017): 491–516.

David, Susan. *Emotional Agility*. New York: Avery, 2016.

Davidson, Richard, and Sharon Begley. *The Emotional Life of Your Brain*. New York: Penguin, 2012.

DeSimone, Melanie. "31 Practical Ways to Love Grieving Families in the First Few Days." *Huffington Post*, February 25, 2016. https://www.huffingtonpost.com/melanie-desimone/31-practical-ways-to-love-grieving-families-in-the-first-few-days_b_9193060.html.

Devine, Megan. "How to Help a Grieving Friend: 11 Things to Do When You're Not Sure What to Do." *Huffington Post*, November 25, 2013. https://www.huffingtonpost.com/megan-devine/death-and-dying_b_4329830.html.

Ehlers, Sharon. *Grief Reiki*. Ferndale, WA: AlyBlue Media, 2016.

Emmons, Robert. *Gratitude Works!* San Francisco: Jossey-Bass, 2013.

Epictetus. *The Art of Living*. Charlotte, NC: Starr Publications, 2017.

Firestone, Robert, Lisa A. Firestone, and Joyce Catlett. *The Self under Siege: Voice Therapy and Differentiation*. New York: Routledge, 2013.

Friday, Paul. *Friday's Laws*. Pittsburgh: Bradley Oak Publications, 1999.

Furey, R. J. *The Joy of Kindness*. New York: Crossroad Publishers, 1993.

Gallo, Amy. "How to Turn a Bad Day Around." *Harvard Business Review*, October 16, 2015.

Goleman, Daniel, and Richard Davidson. *Altered Traits: Science Reveals How Meditation Changes Your Mind, Brain, and Body*. New York: Avery Books, 2017.

Graham, Linda. *Bouncing Back: Rewiring Your Brain for Maximum Resilience and Well-Being*. Novato, CA: New World Library, 2013.

Grubbs, Geri. *Bereavement Dreaming and the Individuating Soul*. Berwick, ME: Nicolas-Hays, Inc., 2004.

Hafner, Katie. "Researchers Confront an Epidemic of Loneliness." *New York Times*, September 5, 2016. https://www.nytimes.com/2016/09/06/health/loneliness-aging-health-effects.html.

Hawkins, David R. *Power vs. Force*. Carlsbad, CA: Hay House Publications, 1995.

Hemingway, Ernest. *A Farewell to Arms*. New York: Scribner and Sons, 1929.

Hensler, Rebecca. "Grief Beyond Belief," 2017. http://www.griefbeyondbelief.org/.

Hoffner, Erik. "As We Lay Dying: Stephen Jenkinson on How We Deny Our Mortality." *The Sun*, August 2015.

Hoge, Elizabeth A., Eric Bui, Sophie A. Palitz, Noah R. Schwarz, Maryann E. Owens, Jennifer M. Johnston, Mark H. Pollack, and Naomi M. Simon. "The Effect of Mindfulness

Meditation Training on Biological Acute Stress Responses in Generalized Anxiety Disorder." *Psychiatry Research*, January 25, 2017. doi:10.1016/j.psychres.2017.01.006.

Hughes, Suzanne. "Project Lost and Found." *Project Lost and Found*, 2017. http://www.projectlostandfound.com/.

Infurna, Frank J., and Suniya S. Luthar. "The Multidimensional Nature of Resilience to Spousal Loss." *Journal of Personality and Social Psychology* 112, no. 6 (2017): 926–47. doi:10.1037/pspp0000095.

Infurna, Frank J., Maja Wiest, Denis Gerstorf, Nilam Ram, Jürgen Schupp, Gert G. Wagner, and Jutta Heckhausen. "Changes in Life Satisfaction When Losing One's Spouse: Individual Differences in Anticipation, Reaction, Adaptation and Longevity in the German Socio-Economic Panel Study (SOEP)." *Ageing and Society* 37, no. 5 (May 2017): 899–934. doi:10.1017/S0144686X15001543.

Joseph, Stephen, ed. *Positive Psychology in Practice: Promoting Human Flourishing in Work, Health, Education, and Everyday Life*. Second edition. Hoboken, NJ: Wiley, 2015.

———. *What Doesn't Kill Us: The New Psychology of Posttraumatic Growth*. New York: Basic Books, 2011.

Jung, Carl. *The Collected Works of C.G. Jung: The Structure and Dynamics of the Psyche*. Vol. 16. Princeton, NJ: Princeton University Press, 1970.

———. *Memories, Dreams, Reflections*. New York: Pantheon Books/Random House, 1963.

Kabat-Zinn, Jon. "Mindfulness Apps with Jon Kabat-Zinn," 2017. http://mindfulness apps.com/.

———. *Mindfulness for Beginners*. Boulder, CO: Sounds True, 2012.

———. "Mindfulness Meditation—Guided Mindfulness Meditation Practices with Jon Kabat-Zinn," 2017. https://www.mindfulnesscds.com/.

Kashdan, Todd. *Curious?* New York: Harper Collins, 2009.

Katie, Byron. *Loving What Is*. New York: Three Rivers Press, 2002.

King, Laura A., Samantha J. Heintzelman, and Sarah J. Ward. "Beyond the Search for Meaning: A Contemporary Science of the Experience of Meaning in Life." *Current Directions in Psychological Science* 25, no. 4 (August 1, 2016): 211–16. doi:10.1177/0963721416656354.

Kini, Prathik, Joel Wong, Sydney McInnis, Nicole Gabana, and Joshua W. Brown. "The Effects of Gratitude Expression on Neural Activity." *NeuroImage* 128 (March 2016): 1–10. doi:10.1016/j.neuroimage.2015.12.040.

Klass, Dennis, Phyllis Silverman, and Steven Nickman. *Continuing Bonds*. Washington, DC: Taylor and Francis, 1996.

Kübler-Ross, Elisabeth. *On Death and Dying*. New York: Routledge, 1969.

Kushner, Harold. *When Bad Things Happen to Good People*. New York: Schocken Books, 1981.

Lamott, Anne. "It's Been Said That Expectations Are Resentments under Construction." Facebook post, November 5, 2014.

Lathia, Neal, Gillian M. Sandstrom, Cecilia Mascolo, and Peter J. Rentfrow. "Happier People Live More Active Lives: Using Smartphones to Link Happiness and Physical Activity." *PLOS ONE* 12, no. 1 (January 4, 2017): e0160589. doi:10.1371/journal.pone.0160589.

Law, Eleanor, Afaf Girgis, Lambert Sylvie, Janelle Levesque, and Hilda Pickett. "Telomeres and Stress: Promising Avenues for Research in Psycho-Oncology." *Asia-Pacific Journal of Oncology Nursing* 3, no. 2 (2016): 137–47. doi:10.4103/2347-5625.182931.

Lesser, Elizabeth. *Broken Open*. New York: Villard Books, 2005.

Levine, Stephen. *A Year to Live: How to Live This Year as If It Were Your Last*. New York: Crown Publishing, 1997.

Lewis, C. S. *A Grief Observed*. New York: Harper and Row, 1961.

Lu, Stacy. "How Chronic Stress Is Harming Our DNA." *Monitor on Psychology* 45, no. 9 (2014): 28.

Lutgendorf, Susan K., and Barbara L. Andersen. "Biobehavioral Approaches to Cancer Progression and Survival: Mechanisms and Interventions." *The American Psychologist* 70, no. 2 (March 2015): 186–97. doi:10.1037/a0035730.

Marcus, C. C. *House as a Mirror of Self: Exploring the Deeper Meaning of Home*. Newbury-port, MA: Conari Press, 1995.

Martin, Joel W., and Patricia Romanowski. *Love Beyond Life: The Healing Power of After-Death Communication*. New York: Harper Collins, 2008.

McAdams, Dan. *The Redemptive Self*. New York: Oxford University Press, 2006.

McKinley, T. "There Is Nothing You Can Say to Heal Someone Else's Grief." *The Mighty*, December 5, 2016. https://themighty.com/2016/12/what-to-say-to-someone-whos-grieving/.

Miller, Richard. *The iRest Program for Healing PTSD: A Proven Effective Approach to Using Yoga Nidra Meditation and Deep Relaxation to Overcome Trauma*. Oakland, CA: New Harbinger Publications, 2015.

———. *Resting in Stillness*. San Rafael, CA: Integrative Restoration Institute, 2011.

———. *Yoga Nidra: A Meditative Practice for Deep Relaxation and Healing*. Boulder, CO: Sounds True, 2005.

Mills, Paul J., Laura Redwine, Kathleen Wilson, Meredith A. Pung, Kelly Chinh, Barry H. Greenberg, Ottar Lunde, et al. "The Role of Gratitude in Spiritual Well-Being in Asymptomatic Heart Failure Patients." *Spirituality in Clinical Practice (Washington, D.C.)* 2, no. 1 (March 2015): 5–17. doi:10.1037/scp0000050.

Mincolla, Mark. *Whole Health*. New York: Tarcher/Penguin, 2013.

Mojo Creations. "Mojo. Fitness for the Soul." *Mojo Creations*, 2015. http://mojocreations.com/.

Nemzoff, Ruth. *Don't Bite Your Tongue: How to Foster Rewarding Relationships with Your Adult Children*. New York: St. Martin's Griffin, 2008.

Nepo, Mark. *The Book of Awakening*. San Francisco: Conari Press, 2011.

Newman, Kira. "Five Science-Based Strategies for More Happiness." *Greater Good Science Center*, March 16, 2016.

Nhat Hanh, Thich. *Fear: Essential Wisdom for Getting Through the Storm*. New York: Harper Collins, 2012.

Nichols, Wallace. *Blue Mind*. New York: Little, Brown and Company, 2014.

Norcross, John. *Changeology*. New York: Simon and Schuster, 2012.

Nouwen, Henri. *Out of Solitude*. Notre Dame, IN: Ave Maria Press, 2004.

Oaklander, Mandy. "Bounce Back." *Time*, June 1, 2015.

Oliver, Laura. *The Story Within: New Insights and Inspiration for Writers*. New York: Penguin, 2011.

O'Rourke, Meghan. "Good Grief." *The New Yorker*, January 25, 2010. https://www.newyorker.com/magazine/2010/02/01/good-grief.

Ostaseski, Frank. *The Five Invitations: Discovering What Death Can Teach Us About Living Fully*. First edition. New York: Flatiron Books, 2017.

Parkes, C. Murray. "Determinants of Outcome Following Bereavement." *OMEGA—Journal of Death and Dying* 6, no. 4 (January 1, 1976): 303–23. doi:10.2190/PR0R-GLPD-5FPB-422L.

Pearlman, Laurie A. *Treating Traumatic Bereavement: A Practitioner's Guide*. New York: The Guilford Press, 2014.

Pennebaker, James. *Writing to Heal*. Oakland, CA: New Harbinger Publications, 2004.

Pert, Candace. *Molecules of Emotion: The Science Behind Mind-Body Medicine*. New York: Touchstone, 1999.

Pietromonaco, Paula R., and Nancy L. Collins. "Interpersonal Mechanisms Linking Close Relationships to Health." *The American Psychologist* 72, no. 6 (September 2017): 531–42. doi:10.1037/amp0000129.

Pirraglia, Paul A., John M. Hampton, Allison B. Rosen, and Whitney P. Witt. "Psychological Distress and Trends in Healthcare Expenditures and Outpatient Healthcare." *The American Journal of Managed Care* 17, no. 5 (May 2011): 319–28.

Remen, Rachel. *Kitchen Table Wisdom*. New York: Riverhead Books, 1996.

Rendon, Jim. *Upside: The New Science of Post-Traumatic Growth*. New York: Touchstone, 2015.

Rook, Karen S., and Susan T. Charles. "Close Social Ties and Health in Later Life: Strengths and Vulnerabilities." *The American Psychologist* 72, no. 6 (September 2017): 567–77. doi:10.1037/amp0000104.

Sapolsky, Robert M. *Behave: The Biology of Humans at Our Best and Worst*. New York: Penguin Press, 2017.

Savage, Margaret V. "Unpublished Note," 2011.

———. "Unpublished Poem Written by Sherry's Sister 02/19/1942–01/02/2017," 2006.

Schmoldt, A., H. F. Benthe, and G. Haberland. "Digitoxin Metabolism by Rat Liver Microsomes." *Biochemical Pharmacology* 24, no. 17 (September 1, 1975): 1639–41.

Schubert, Christine F., Ulrike Schmidt, and Rita Rosner. "Posttraumatic Growth in Populations with Posttraumatic Stress Disorder—A Systematic Review on Growth-Related Psychological Constructs and Biological Variables." *Clinical Psychology and Psychotherapy* 23, no. 6 (November 2016): 469–86. doi:10.1002/cpp.1985.

Servan-Schreiber, David. *Anticancer*. New York: Penguin, 2008.

Shear, M. Katherine, Charles F. Reynolds, Naomi M. Simon, Sidney Zisook, Yuanjia Wang, Christine Mauro, Naihua Duan, Barry Lebowitz, and Natalia Skritskaya. "Optimizing Treatment of Complicated Grief: A Randomized Clinical Trial." *JAMA Psychiatry* 73, no. 7 (July 1, 2016): 685–94. doi:10.1001/jamapsychiatry.2016.0892.

Sifferlin, Alexandra. "The Healing Power of Nature." *Time*, July 13, 2016.

Silverman, Phyllis, and Madelyn Kelly. *A Parent's Guide to Raising Grieving Children*. New York: Oxford University Press, 2009.

Sleek, Scott. "The Long and the Short of It." *APS Observer* 27, no. 9 (October 31, 2014). https://www.psychologicalscience.org/observer/the-long-and-the-short-of-it.

Spring, Bonnie, Abby C. King, Sherry L. Pagoto, Linda Van Horn, and Jeffery D. Fisher. "Fostering Multiple Healthy Lifestyle Behaviors for Primary Prevention of Cancer." *The American Psychologist* 70, no. 2 (March 2015): 75–90. doi:10.1037/a0038806.

Strom, Max. *There Is No App for Happiness*. New York: Skyhorse Publishing, 2013.

Tatelbaum, Judy. *The Courage to Grieve*. New York: Lippincott and Crowell, 1980.

Taylor, Jill Bolte. *My Stroke of Insight*. New York: Viking, 2006.

Tedeschi, Richard G., and Lawrence G. Calhoun. "The Posttraumatic Growth Inventory: Measuring the Positive Legacy of Trauma." *Journal of Traumatic Stress* 9, no. 3 (January 1, 1996): 455–71. doi:10.1002/jts.2490090305.

Tedeschi, Richard G., and Bret A. Moore. *The Posttraumatic Growth Workbook: Coming through Trauma Wiser, Stronger, and More Resilient*. Oakland, CA: New Harbinger Publications, 2016.

Tolle, Eckhart. *A New Earth: Awakening to Your Life's Purpose*. New York: Penguin, 2005.

Turner, Kelly. *Radical Remission*. New York: Harper Collins, 2014.

Uchino, Bert N., Richard M. Cawthon, Timothy W. Smith, Kathleen C. Light, Justin McKenzie, McKenzie Carlisle, Heather Gunn, Wendy Birmingham, and Kimberly Bowen. "Social Relationships and Health: Is Feeling Positive, Negative, or Both (Ambivalent) About Your Social Ties Related to Telomeres?" *Health Psychology: Official Journal of the Division of Health Psychology, American Psychological Association* 31, no. 6 (November 2012): 789–96. doi:10.1037/a0026836.

University of Wisconsin–Madison. "Science Overview—Center for Healthy Minds," 2017. https://centerhealthyminds.org/science/overview.

Viorst, Judy. *Necessary Losses*. New York: The Free Press, 1986.

Walker, Val. *The Art of Comforting*. New York: Tarcher/Penguin, 2010.

Walsh, Roger. "Lifestyle and Mental Health." *The American Psychologist* 66, no. 7 (October 2011): 579–92. doi:10.1037/a0021769.

Warnick, Melody. *This Is Where You Belong*. New York: Viking, 2016.

Warren, Rick. *The Purpose Driven Life*. Grand Rapids, MI: Zondervan, 2012.

Weller, Francis. *The Wild Edge of Sorrow*. Berkeley, CA: North Atlantic Books, 2015.

Williams, Florence. *The Nature Fix: Why Nature Makes Us Happier, Healthier, and More Creative*. First edition. New York: Norton, 2017.

Williams, Margery. *The Velveteen Rabbit*. New York: George H. Duran Co., 1922.

Wood, Alex M., Jeffrey J. Froh, and Adam W. A. Geraghty. "Gratitude and Well-Being: A
    Review and Theoretical Integration." *Clinical Psychology Review* 30, no. 7 (November
    2010): 890–905. doi:10.1016/j.cpr.2010.03.005.
Wortman, Camille B. "Posttraumatic Growth: Progress and Problems." *Psychological In-
    quiry* 15, no. 1 (2004): 81–90.

INDEX

AARP Connect2Affect site, 81
Abbey (author's dog), 83–84
Achor, Shawn, 102–103
acupuncture, 9, 45, 52, 107, 109, 125
Affordable Care Act, 108
afterlife, concept of, 46
Altered Traits (Goleman and Davidson), 99
Altucher, James, 111
American Psychological Association on Palliative Care and End-of-Life Issues, 22
Andrews, Ted, 41
Animal Speak (Andrews), 41
Annapolis, Maryland, 18, 49, 59; cottage description of, 60–61; group joining in, 71, 72; loneliness bouts in, 69–70; meeting new friends in, 71–72; online dating in, 72–74; as overregulated state, 67; people connecting in, 69; real estate exploring in, 60; sea glass collecting and renewal in, 72; writing project seeking in, 74–75
Annapolis Connections Over Coffee, 71
Anticancer (Servan-Schreiber), 126
The Art of Comforting (Walker), 116
Association of Death Education Counselors, 109

Bill and Melinda Gates Foundation, 108
Blackburn, Elizabeth, 79–80

Bonhoeffer, Dietrich, 96
Boss, Pauline, 95, 100–101
Botti, Chris, 23, 137
Bowen, Murray, 92
Bratman, Gregory, 104
Breathe2Relax app, 99
Broken Open (Lesser), 96
Brooks, Arthur C., 103
Brown, Brené, 128
Burchard, Brendon, 98

Calhoun, Lawrence, 62, 63
Calm.com, 99
CAM. *See* complementary and alternative medicine
Cameron, Julia, 107, 111
Campbell, Joseph, 57
cancer, 1–2, 19; additional opinions recommendation for, 129–130; attentiveness and luck in, 12, 128–129; body attention and relevant screenings for, 129; environmental and nutritional exposures contribution to, 126; epidemic of, 123–124; financial resources concerning, 125; hospital advocate in, 131; interpersonal conflict and internal stressors exposure factor in, 126; lifestyle changes focus of, 132; lifestyle factors risk in, 124–125; mind-body-spirit role in, 128; monitoring advocate for, 130–131; negative

interpersonal relationships in, 127; social relationships and loneliness in, 126–127; stress and illness impacting, 124; thoughts and feelings influencing, 127–128; trust instincts and wisdom in, 131. *See also* esophageal cancer

Carnes, Donna, 95, 100–101

Carstensen, Laura, 125

Catlett, Joyce, 92

Center for Complicated Grief, Columbia University, 109

Charles, Susan, 82–83

chemotherapy, 15, 17; emotional side effects of, 21; Jay's break from, 23–24; toxicity of, 21

Chinese medicine, 9, 41

Chodron, Pema, viii–ix, 88

Chopra, Deepak, 46, 123

Chris (author's son-in-law), 18, 28

Christiane (author's daughter), 31, 33, 60–61

Clark, Ramsey, 65

CNP. *See* Constructive Narrative Perspective

Collins, Nancy, 127

colonoscopy, 5–7, 7–8, 106, 129

The Compassionate Friends online support group, 108

complementary and alternative medicine (CAM), 86

complicated grief, 108–109

connect2affect.org, 81

connection, viii, 1, 2, 44–45, 50, 69, 136

Constructive Narrative Perspective (CNP), 90

Cormier, Sherry (author): birth-chart reading and location analysis report for, 60; as contemplating change, 59–61; Dad final visit of, 19–20; essential identity loss of, 34–35; fear and grief of, 34; friends and family debriefing of, 32–33; friendships need of, 59; grief journey impact on, 53; individuation growth of, 54; Jay saving obsession of, 52; mother's spirit manifestations of, 54–55; psychic intuitive reading for, 46–47; Renaissance angel picture impact on, 34

cranial sacral therapy, 45, 52

cumulative grief, 109–110

Curious? (Kashdan), 84

Dalai Lama, 89

David, Susan, 100

Davidson, Richard, 98, 99, 100, 102

DeSimone, Melanie, 115

Devine, Megan, 115

Dick's Sporting Goods, 23

Die Wise (Jenkinson), 114

Don't Bite Your Tongue: How to Foster Rewarding Relationships with Your Adult Children (Nemzoff), 83

Emmons, Robert, 103

emotion, 30–31, 45, 79, 95–96; chemotherapy side effects on, 21; expectations role in, 88–89; Friday's Law use for, 12; friends role importance in, 9; hospital feeling management of, 11; impermanence and suffering concepts in, 88; letting go of, 89; managing challenge of, 8–9; mind-body link in illness and, 52; physiology impact of, 88; regulation of, 88; talking with others as management of, 11–12; unforgettable conversation regarding, 8

endoscopy, 5, 6, 129

Epel, Elissa, 79–80

Epictetus, 88, 132–133

esophageal cancer, 1, 5, 7, 10, 11, 14; Internet information availability on, 11, 84; luck in treatment of, 12, 128–129; rise of, 5, 123; roller-coaster ride of, 12–14

exercise, 80, 98; in comprehensive cancer treatment programs, 22; for grief survivors, 99; for stress reduction, 80–81

Fast, Jay Howard, 52, 68–69; active dying phase of, 31; Annapolis trip meltdown of, 18; birthday celebration of, 10; blessing and prayer for, 32; book of Job dream including, 42–43; buffalo dream concerning, 40–41; cancer diagnosis of, 1–2; chemo break of, 23–24; chemo emotional side effects of, 21; chemo treatments and energy of, 17; client understanding and connecting capacity of, 136; colonoscopy and endoscopy of, 5–6; colonoscopy and endoscopy results of, 6–7, 7–8; on control, 138–139; deteriorating condition of, 27; different house dream with, 49; emotional health of, 30–31; end-of-life care decision for, 29–30; final visit home for, 30; as first-class romantic, 136–137, 137–138; full-day chemotherapy treatments and plan for, 15; generosity of, 137; granddaughter visit with, 17–18; initial treatment transformation of, 16; large schooner dream with, 111; Lee cancer support dinner with, 19; less frequent dreams about, 53; love affirmation of, 30; medical research donation of, 32, 37; memorial service for, 37–38; no demons anymore dream with, 43–44; pericardium procedure of, 28–29; photodynamic therapy procedure of, 24; procedures and scans results of, 12–13; and psychic intuitive, 46–47; Reiki session message of, 45–46; relationship with, 1; resourcefulness of, 137; resurrection dream with, 47–48; shadow side of, 52; short weekend travel of, 17; spiritual journey of, 51, 52; spiritual rehabilitation dream with, 44–45; Starfish cottage dreams about, 49–51; Thanksgiving holiday with, 23; transitioning of, 31–32; treatment plan for, 13–14; unprocessed grief of, 52; UPMC consultation of, 10–12; UPMC three-month follow-up of, 22–23; warmth of, 135; what's it like to die? dream about, 48; WVU cancer center admission of, 28; WVU cancer center meeting of, 14

Fear: Essential Wisdom for Getting Through the Storm (Thich Nhat Hanh), 51

Firestone, Lisa A., 92

Firestone, Robert, 92

forest bathing, 104

form manifestations, 54–55; bed vibrations and, 38; cards and notes as, 38–39; during memorial service, 38

Friday, Paul, 5, 12

Friday's Laws (Friday), 12

friends, 9, 32–33, 59, 71–72

Gallo, Amy, 102

Ghost, 37

GI screening, 5

Goleman, Daniel, 99

Graham, Linda, 86–87

gratitude, 87, 102–103

grief, 34, 53; African and Hispanic Americans rituals of, 117; assumptive world concept in, 70; attachment theory in, 70; Buddhist mustard seed story of, viii; children relationships during, 82–83; Christian rituals for, 116; complicated, 108–109; continuing bonds in, 69; continuum evolvement of, 2; cumulative, 109–110; dark night of soul in, 42, 43; ebbs and flows of, 76; European American cultural groups ritual of, 117; firsthand experience in, vii; gap staying in, 96–97; honoring of, 76–77; illiteracy of, 114; intellectual self-care in, 84–85; Jenkinson on, 114; Jewish ritual for, 117; journey with, 2, 2–3; lifetime of homesickness in, 75; low spot in, 41–42; Native and Asian American cultural rituals of, 117; Roman Catholic Christian rituals for, 116–117; sadness as human emotion in, 95–96; as sneaky, 75–76; stage theory of, 76; strangers kindness in, 7; survivor struggle with, 55; Thich Nhat Hanh journey of, 54; time and space in, 121–122; as traumatic stress, 79; unprocessed, 52; variety of experiences in, 2; volunteering as spiritual practice for, 71

grief helpers: acknowledgment of situation as, 114; awkwardness of, 113–114; calling and planning responsibility of, 115; concrete offers from, 115; cultural and ethnic and religious groups impact of, 116–117; despondency and hopelessness cues

alertness of, 121; effective, 114; emotionally charged words comfortability of, 119; expectation loss for, 119; fixing avoidance as, 118; gifts suitability of, 121; griever cues noticing of, 120; hard day asking of, 121; helpful presence of, 115–116; offer follow through of, 120; open-ended questions as, 114; person-to-person contact as, 118; platitudes avoidance as, 119; prepare yourself as, 118; response range of, 113; sorrow sharing of, 116; support offer from, 120; unfinished feelings of, 116
grief rituals, 101, 116–117
grief survivors, 55; closure myth in, 95; contribution and service for, 101–102; cumulative grief of, 109–110; damaging messages and negativity in, 97–98; doubler activity for, 102; exercise and sleep and nutrition for, 99; gap staying of, 96–97; gratitude journaling for, 103; gratitude practice for, 102–103; intention creation of, 97–98; meaning search of, 100–101; meditation for, 98–99; nature connection aiding, 103–104; random acts of kindness by, 101–102; recommendations for responding to, 117–121; resilience seed planting of, 98; rituals regarding, 101; sadness as human emotion of, 95–96; social support for, 100; volunteering and mentoring tools of, 101
Grover (fictitious name of UPMC oncologist), 13, 22, 24
Grubbs, Geri, 39, 47, 50, 51

The Happiness Advantage (Achor), 102
HeadSpace app, 99
The Healing Power of Nature (Sifferlin), 104
Hemingway, Ernest, 95
Hensler, Rebecca, 108
Hoffner, Erik, 110, 114
House as a Mirror of Self (Marcus), 49
Hughes, Suzanne, 106–107
Hurricane Irene, 65

individuation, 54
in-home hospice, adverse experience with, 20, 29
InsightTimer app, 99
Integrative Restorative Institute, 86
Iyengar, B. K. S., 81

Jack (fictitious name of friend), 5, 7, 15, 30, 31, 32
Janus, 31
Jay. See Fast, Jay Howard
Jenkinson, Stephen, 110, 114
Joan (fictitious name of friend), 5, 7, 15, 30, 31, 32
Joseph, Stephen, 62, 64
Jung, Carl, 1, 40, 42
Just Say Hello campaign, 81

Kabat-Zinn, Jon, 99
Kashdan, Todd, 84
Katie, Byron, 30, 111, 128
Kennedy, Ted, 47, 48
Kini, Prathik, 103
Kitchen Table Wisdom (Remen), 132
Kübler-Ross, Elisabeth, 76
Kushner, Harold, 91

Laghari (fictitious name of oncology head resident at WVU Cancer Center), 28, 31
Lamott, Anne, 75, 88–89
Lao Tzu, 88
Laozi, 90
Laura (Jay's daughter), 5, 24, 32, 50
Lee (fictitious name of textbook editor), 19
Lesser, Elizabeth, 96
leukemia, 7, 91, 123
Levine, Stephen, 48
life, 29–30; connection in, 1, 2; delight about, vii; fairytale in, 1, 2; struggling to make a, 57
Lisanne (author's daughter), 18, 33, 38, 48, 73, 82, 83
loneliness: animal companion for, 83–84; as health risk factor, 126–127; higher stress hormones link to, 81; loss and, 81; Maryland bouts of, 69–70; people support list for, 82

loss, 34–35, 63, 119; anger in, 87;
assumptive world concept in, 70;
awkwardness over, 113–114; basic
choices in, 90; bitterness of, 76–77;
children relationships during, 82–83;
closure myth in, 95; CNP approach in,
90–91; connection optimism in, viii;
coping and thriving in, viii; empty
space gift in, 97; gratitude in, 87;
growth and new path from, 58; holding
on to things in, 89; involuntary or
voluntary challenges in, 91–92; letting
go of, 90; loneliness and, 81;
opportunities and growth from, 91; out
of place feeling in, 58–59;
psychologist's perspective on, vii;
social support following, 57–58, 59;
spiritual practices developing for,
85–87; surprising discoveries in, viii; as
traumatic stress, vii, 79; variety of
experiences in, 2; wither or grow from,
vii, viii
loss, coping guidelines for, viii, 104;
comparisons avoidance in, 106;
complicated grief in, 108–109;
counseling in, 108; cumulative grief in,
109–110; disenfranchised grief and
ambiguous loss in, 110; financial
service in, 108; grief triggers plan in,
105; large schooner dream in, 111;
major decisions deferral in, 105;
motivation identification in, 107; new
interest acquisition as, 106; online
support groups in, 108; resource
development and use in, 107–110;
responsibility reduction in, 104–105;
self relationship cultivation in,
110–111; story sharing in, 106–107;
transformational energies recognition
in, 110; unwanted advice resistance as,
105; vulnerabilities identification as,
105–106; writing project for, 107
Loving What Is (Katie), 30

Marcus, C. C., 49
Martin, Joel, 39, 40, 44
Maureen (fictitious name of neighbor),
23, 32

MBSR. See Mindfulness Based Stress
Reduction
McGuire (fictitious name of UPMC
surgeon), 11, 12–13, 28
McKinley, T., 115
meditation, 85; apps for, 99; caveat for,
99; definition of, 99; MBSR as, 99;
resilience developing in, 98–99
Meichenbaum, Donald, 63, 90
Michaud (fictitious name of oncologist at
WVU Cancer Center), 14, 15, 28, 29
The Mighty.com, 115
Miller, Richard, 79, 86
Mincolla, Mark, 124, 127
mind-body-spirit, 52, 128
mindfulness, 22, 80, 85, 91, 99, 117
Mindfulness Based Stress Reduction
(MBSR), 99
Moore, Demi, 37
Morgantown, West Virginia, 10, 13, 28,
46, 59
moving day: backyard explosion on, 66;
fallen tree on, 65–66; Hurricane Irene
on, 65; pottery pineapple smashed in,
65; shelter meaning on, 66–67; tree-
grinder chance meeting on, 67;
turbulence on, 67–68
My Stroke of Insight (Taylor), 98

The Nature Fix (Williams, F.), 104
Necessary Losses (Viorst), 93
Nemzoff, Ruth, 83
Nepo, Mark, 91
Newman, Kira, 101–102, 104
Nouwen, Henri J. M., 113

Oaklander, Mandy, 98–99
Oliver, Laura, 74, 75
online dating: Andrew date regarding,
73–74; divorced and widowed persons
in, 74; feelings about, 72; Fred
relationship in, 74; physical
appearance interest and, 73
O'Rourke, Meghan, 70
Ostaseski, Frank, 118

palliative care, 22, 29–30
Parkes, C. Murray, 70
Pay It Forward app, 102

Pietromonaco, Paula, 127

pleural effusion, 6, 131

posttraumatic growth (PTG), 61; as awakening, 62; extraversion and age in, 64; meaning of, 62; misconceptions of, 62; PTSD and, 64; signposts facilitation for, 62; social environment encouragement in, 63; societal transformation in, 63; traumatic loss type in, 63; valuable vase analogy of, 62–63

Posttraumatic Stress Disorder (PTSD), 64, 86

psychic intuitive, 46–47

psychosocial oncology, 22

PTG. See posttraumatic growth

PTSD. See Posttraumatic Stress Disorder

purple dendrobium orchid plant, 23, 136–137, 137

Reiki, 125; benefits of, 45; emotional or physical ailment use of, 45; Jay message during, 45–46; stress-reduction and relaxation approach of, 45

Remen, Rachel, 132

Renata (fictitious name of widow friend of author), 58, 69–70, 70

Rendon, Jim, 79, 82

Resting in Stillness, 86

Richard (fictitious name of Vedic astrologer), 60

Romanowski, Patricia, 39, 40, 44

Rook, Karen, 82–83

Rumi, 44, 49, 96–97, 100

Sapolsky, Robert, 124

Savage, Margaret V., 27

sea glass collection, 69, 72

self-care, 80; information-seeking in, 84; learning and curiosity for, 84–85; work as distraction for, 84

self-differentiation: expectations and plans in, 93; greater to lesser continuum of, 92; healthy attachment in, 93; meaning of, 92; situations and people in, 92–93; steps for achieving, 92

The Self Under Siege (Firestone, L., Firestone, R., and Catlett), 92

Servan-Schreiber, David, 126

Shear, Katherine, 109

Shelby(granddaughter), 18

Sifferlin, Alexandra, 104

social networks, 80, 126–127; animal companion as, 83–84; developing importance of, 70; general strategy components of, 70–71; people support list for, 82; Warnick guidebook for, 71

Social Security benefits, 107–108

social support, 57–58, 59, 100

soul: dark night in grief of, 42, 43; existence of, 37; visitation dreams connection with, 44, 44–45

spiritual journey, 51; of Jay, 51, 52; karma concept in, 51

spiritual practices, 71, 87; contemplative prayer as, 85; cultural and religious beliefs as, 86; iRest as, 86; mindfulness and meditation as, 85; stress and loss developing of, 85

Stanford Center on Longevity, 125

Starfish cottage: description of, 60–61; dreams about, 49–51; Jay gifts for, 68–69; projects of, 68; sea glass collection in, 69

Steve (Jay's son-in-law), 24, 32

The Story Within (Oliver), 74

stress, chronic, 45, 79, 81, 126; body effects of, 80, 124; cellular deterioration and telomeres in, 79; emotional and physical health problems in, 79; etiology of illness factor of, 124; exercise value for, 80–81; perceptions of, 79; protein and anxiety levels in, 80; ripple effect of, 124; senescence in, 79; spiritual practices developing for, 85–87; sugar impact on, 80; telomeres evidence-based interventions for, 80; vegetable importance in reducing, 80; water intake and, 80

stress reduction, 9; exercise for, 80–81; Reiki approach for, 45

Strom, Max, 110

Swayze, Patrick, 37

Tactical Breather app, 99
Tao Te Ching (Laozi), 90
Tatelbaum, Judy, 52
Taylor, Jill Bolte, 98
Tedeschi, Richard, 62, 63
Teilhard de Chardin, Pierre, 51
The Telomere Effect (Blackburn and Epel), 80
Thich Nhat Hanh, 37, 51, 54, 96
T. J. Maxx, 9, 23
Tolle, Eckhart, 17, 90
Turner, Kelly, 128

University of Maryland, 71
University of Pittsburgh Medical Center (UPMC): compassionate surgeon at, 11, 12; consultation at, 10–12; esophageal cancer center of, 7, 10; Jay's photodynamic therapy procedure at, 24; Jay's three-month follow-up at, 22–23
The Uplifter app, 103
UPMC. *See* University of Pittsburgh Medical Center
Upside (Rendon), 79, 82

The Velveteen Rabbit (Williams, M.), 135, 138
Veterans Affairs Department, U.S., 22
Viorst, Judith, 93
visitation dreams, 53, 111; abandonment healing in, 41; "big dream" in, 40; book of Job dream as, 42–43; buffalo dream as, 40–41; buffalo symbolism in, 41; characteristics of, 40; deceased relationship in, 47; definition of, 39; different house dream as, 49; frequency vibration in, 42; healing and guiding of, 53; house symbol in, 49; of Jung, 40; Martin and Romanowski on enhancing, 39; messages in, 44, 48, 51; no demons anymore dream as, 43–44; reappearance of, 53; religious or spiritual message in, 43; resurrection dream as, 47–48; sea representation in, 51; soul connection in, 44–45; soul-to-soul contact in, 44; spiritual development level in, 48; spiritual rehabilitation dream as, 44–45; Starfish cottage dreams as, 49–51; suffering meaning in, 42–43; unbroken connection in, 50; what's it like to die? dream as, 48
volunteering, 71, 101, 102

Walker, Val, 116, 120, 121
Walsh, Roger, 132
Warnick, Melody, 71
Warren, Rick, 106
water proximity health benefit, 59–60
Weller, Francis, 116
West Virginia University Cancer Center (WVU), 28; full-day chemotherapy treatments at, 15; GI oncologist at, 14; palliative care unit at, 29–30; physicians clinical expertise at, 28
When I Fall in Love, 23
When Things Fall Apart: Heart Advice for Difficult Times (Chodron), viii–ix, 88
Whole Foods, 23
Williams, Florence, 104
Williams, Margery, 135, 138
Winfrey, Oprah, 81, 103
WVU. *See* West Virginia University Cancer Center

yoga, 99, 107; classes, 7, 59, 69; restorative, 81

ABOUT THE AUTHOR

Sherry Cormier, PhD, is a licensed psychologist and professor emerita in the Department of Counseling, Rehabilitation Counseling, and Counseling Psychology at West Virginia University. She was in private practice in adult psychotherapy in Morgantown, West Virginia, and a former faculty member at the University of Tennessee. She is the author of two textbooks, and she is a certified bereavement trauma specialist and resides in Annapolis, Maryland.